"HOW TO TIP A POOL CUE"

The Laymen's Guide

By

TERRY MACIOGE

ISBN: 1-4107-7730-8 (e-book)
ISBN: 1-4107-7731-6 (Paperback)

Library of Congress Control Number: 2003095010

This book is printed on acid free paper.

Printed in the United States of America
Bloomington, IN

Book and Cover Design by
Terry Macioge

Tool and Clamping Methods Illustrated by
Walter Albee

1stBooks – rev. 08/29/03

ACKNOWLEDGEMENTS

I would like to personally thank Mr. Joe Porper and the late Mr. James Willard for their years of contribution to this sport, and for their many billiard tipping tools and maintenance tool designs.

Thanks to Patricia Sheldon, Willard's daughter, for allowing me to use the form designed by her Father, to explain the proper technique, for shaping the tip on a cue.

This author would like to thank Mr. Barry Szamboti for his input and the time, during my visit, to talk about the tip, and its replacement. Getting his recommendations and input is greatly appreciated.

Thanks to Robert Byrne for his recommendations and suggestions to resources.

My thanks to "Billiards Digest," several of the Internet Site owners, and the cue manufacturing companies, Wholesalers and Distributors who have supported me in my endeavor and provided information and encouragement.

DEDICATION

This guide is dedicated to the many billiard players/novice/laymen who have never been able to replace a tip on a cue stick and make it stay.

It is dedicated to the many satisfied customers/friends who I have assisted, over the years, who encouraged me to write the procedure, for them.

It is dedicated to my friend Walter, who for over fifty years of love for this game, has contributed to the knowledge of the game, its sales and service, and the techniques he used for repairing cue tips.

PHOTOS/GRAPHICS

A very special thanks to Mr. Rory Mueller, of "Mueller Recreational Products," for his cooperation and assistance in supplying photography and descriptions for many of the tools, tips and supplies shown in this book.

To Jay "Eli" Tuttle, a promising architecture student at Philadelphia University, for his time in preparing the graphics presented in this book. A special thanks, to my son Matt, for his graphic work and my daughter Danielle, for all her assistance, on the photography.

Thanks to Mr. Don Spetkar, of Adams Ltd, for supplying the art work for tip items carried by his company, and to Tony Kalamdaryn of Tiger Products for his photo of the New Sniper Tip.

Finally, my thanks to Tony Long, "Mr. Billiards," Doug Mitchell and Patty Zimmerman, of Billiards Express, for the use of the Tip Pik, on the cover and in the book and for permission to use the "Cue Stick Grooming and Maintenance" instructions.

TABLE OF CONTENTS

PREFACE

Congratulations, as a novice, you have just made a wise purchase. By the time you read "How to Tip a Pool Cue," "The Laymen's Guide" and tipped your first cue, you will have recovered the cost you paid for this book.

To my knowledge, there is no book currently available on the market that details a step-by-step procedure of instruction, on how to replace a worn cue tip, on a billiard cue stick. I could never understand why no one has taken the time, in this popular sport, to write a book, on what is considered the most important part of the billiard cue. I guess they were waiting for me to do it. I am not the authority on tipping cues, but I have enough experience at it, that I believe I can outline the process for you to be able to do it successfully.

This book represents one laymen's method using several manual techniques, with no machinery, like used at cue manufacturers or custom cue makers. It will include pictorial views, to describe the process and show the steps involved. It is by no means the authoritative technique. There are others. I believe you will find it a good alternative to sending your shafts away for repair or having someone replace the tip for you.

I have had many customers ask me to replace their tip. Many have tried and many have failed. After you have reviewed what I have to say, you will realize there is more to replacing a tip than just gluing it on top of the ferrule. There are plenty of books for sale that tell you how to play the various pool games, how to make shots, how to buy a cue, the history of billiards, how to do trick shots, how to value the price of a cue, but none I know of, that provide the simple maintenance instructions for a tip and instructions on how to replace the tip, both of which are important, for you to maintain a consistent game of pool.

I am sure those who have done tip repairs have a technique or procedure that might differ from mine. The contents of this book represent the techniques I use that have been successful. You may use them, alter them or choose not to use them. You may decide to continue paying someone else to replace your tip. Or, it may be, you just do not feel confident in doing it yourself. Hopefully, we will overcome the feeling of being unsure at doing it, to a confident feeling of certainty, that you can do it.

The material in "How to Tip a Pool Cue" comes from many sources. It comes from my involvement with the sport over many years. I have watched others who have tipped cues and have benefited from their knowledge. While managing a Billiard Store, I tipped thousands of cues giving me exposure to the industry. I assisted in the buying and selling of cues, evaluated cues for an import distributor and learned about the construction of cues from various cue manufacturers, custom cue makers and going to the shows. The knowledge I gained, has added to my understanding of repair techniques used in tipping the cue. By the time you read this guide, my secret of how to glue a tip on without having it fall off, on the first attempt, will be answered. If followed properly, you will never have to worry about long waits to get your tip replaced. When you have a game or are in need of your cue stick that night, you will be prepared to handle the task of replacing a worn or missing tip. Most novice players only own one good cue stick and cannot afford to be without it.

I have spoken with many players over the years and although it is hard to believe, many do not know, there are tools available, to provide maintenance, to the cue tip or the procedure on how to replace it. I hope to add enough information for you to be successful at replacing your own cue tip with confidence and have a better understanding and appreciation for the most important part of the cue.

I will discus tools, techniques and some of the supplies that are available, to make tipping a cue and maintaining your tip, an easy task.

INTRODUCTION

This book has been developed at the request of many billiard players and friends, who from time to time have had a need to re-tip their billiard cue sticks. After years of tipping cues for many billiard players, I have constantly been asked, "Why don't you write a book and explain how you tip a pool cue?" So here it is, for all of you, who have made this request of me, over the years.

I hope you will find it informative, simple and explained in terms that even the novice player can understand. I use pictures to show the tools, and the steps in the repair process. I am a firm believer in the saying that "a picture is worth a thousand words."

The photos will show each step of the replacement process. I have provided a list of the equipment, sources, and various products that you might use to accomplish replacement of the tip on your cue stick.

This book is for those of us who cannot afford to have a professional cue maker replace our tips or afford the $10- $40 fee that is usually assessed for the labor and tip. It will eliminate the need to ship your cue away for weeks at a time. The inconvenience, of having to be without your cue, will be eliminated. Hopefully, with a little practice and following the instructions, you will be able to replace your cue tip and enjoy playing the game.

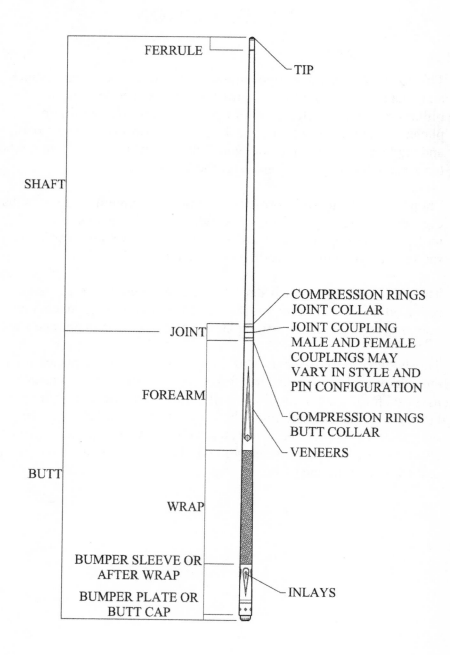

FERRULE

TIP

SHAFT

COMPRESSION RINGS
JOINT COLLAR

JOINT

JOINT COUPLING
MALE AND FEMALE
COUPLINGS MAY
VARY IN STYLE AND
PIN CONFIGURATION

FOREARM

COMPRESSION RINGS
BUTT COLLAR

VENEERS

BUTT

WRAP

BUMPER SLEEVE OR
AFTER WRAP

INLAYS

BUMPER PLATE OR
BUTT CAP

CHAPTER I

TOOLS AND EQUIPMENT

DETERMINING THE ARC

MAINTAINING THE ARC

WHEN TO CHANGE THE TIP

MAINTENANCE TOOLS

THE CLAMPS

Chapter I

The Tools You'll Need

How to Determine the Arc and Maintain It

In this chapter we will discus some of the many types of tools available on the market for maintaining and replacing a cue tip.

If not for the French Infantryman Captain Francois Mingaud, who while he was being held as a political prisoner, discovered the first leather cue tip, and changed the course of billiard history, we would not be talking about the maintenance or replacement of the tip today. Mike Shamos points out in his book "The New Illustrated Encyclopedia of Billiards," page 259, the first tip was cut from a leather harness. The exact date of this invention is not certain. In Mike's book he indicates a period somewhere between 1807 and 1823 and most likely closer to 1818 as indicated by the notes left in Mingaud's handwriting. Robert Byrne, however, in his book "Byrne's New Standard Book of Pool and Billiards," page 40, puts the date in or around 1807. In any event, the invention by Mingaud, has changed the way pool has been played since that time. Captain Mingaud was able with his new leather tip to apply so much spin on the cue ball that people believed he was some kind of a sorcerer. He made some amazing shots that even today would be considered very difficult. Shortly after, around 1820 Bartley and Carr of Bath, England gave us their invention, the chalk. This is referred to in "Byrne's New Standard Book of Pool and Billiards" also on page 40. One can only imagine what Captain Mingaud was able to do with his leather tip after applying chalk. To date, there has not been an invention that has superceded the combination of leather and chalk. Since the invention of chalk, much has been learned, about its effects and how to apply it. Today, we know a properly shaped tip is key to playing consistently and the tip must be well chalked. Eventually the tip, from shaping and

3

Terry Macioge

wear, will need routine maintenance and sooner or later will need to be replaced.

Before you begin attempting to replace your cue tip, you should know how to determine if it needs replaced. When should it be replaced? How will we replace the tip? And, what shape should a tip have? What tools and equipment are needed to accomplish this task?

If a tip mushrooms or expands over the side of your cue's ferrule, flattens out, there are tools you can use to reshape the tip before replacing it. I have listed some of these tools, which should become part of the accessories you carry in your cue bag. You may not need every tool, but it is important that you at least have a shaper, a tip pik and a scuffer and maybe a type of burnisher. The multi-functional tools like the Ulti-Mate or Stubby are good ways to start. You should own a minimum of one of the first three items. Some tools are designed to perform multiple functions while others perform only one specific function.

Some of the popular tools are:

-The **Stubby**, a tool that does three things to the tip. It is **a shaper,** meaning it will provide the arc you need on your tip, it is **a scuffer**, which adds texture to the tip, and it is a **burnisher,** it will reshape a mushroomed tip. The scuffer can also be used as a tapper the same as a tip tapper tool. Some models have a shaker on one end, which contains enough hand chalk stored, for a night of pool playing. This tool will also seat your chalk with a tap or roll of the tapper end. If available, in your area, I would recommend picking one up as the get started tool.

4

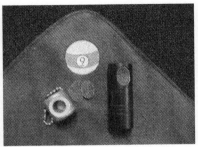

Stubby

Here is a brief explanation of what each process is meant to do.

The **Shaper** can be used to round off the leather tip and regain the arc. A severely mushroomed tip, which has flattened, should be burnished first, to try and reshape the tip, as much as possible. If it cannot be completely reshaped with the burnishing tool, it will require the blade tool to cut off the excess that might still be mushroomed over the edge of the ferrule. Using softer leathered tips will tend to cause this condition. Every time you use a shaper to restore the shape of your tip, you will lose some of the leather. Tip replacement will eventually occur as a result of constant reshaping. It should also be noted, the more your tip flattens or mushrooms, the more frequently mushrooming will occur.

A **tip burnisher,** like the one sold by Joe Porper, causes friction with a fast motion that draws the leather of the tip upward. Putting the tip into the burnisher and turning it, creates a friction that will help to reshape the tip to its original form. The excess can be eliminated with the cutting tool or the shaper by turning it to one side to rasp off the excess leather or cutting it with the reshaping tool.

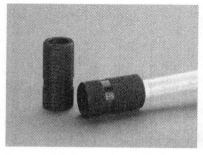

Tip Burnisher

The **scuffers,** like the universal Willard tapper, the Ulti-Mate, Cube, and other similar tools provide ways to scuff the tip. Usually a tool made of metal filings or a corrugated file metal, used to rough up, remove the coatings and shape the leather, in order to be able to seat the chalk. Scuff it back and forth to bring up the nap of the leather. These little naps hold the chalk to the tip of your cue. This is important for chalking a cue and seating the chalk for best action. Remove the excess chalk with a slight tap on the palm of your hand or blowing it off. **Caution**, Do Not let the excess chalk from the tip fall on the felt tablecloth, by tapping over the table or on the rail of the table. Chalk build up on felt can cause distortions in shots. It does not take much distortion to cause you to miss a shot.

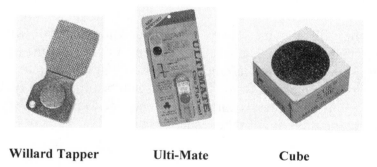

Willard Tapper   **Ulti-Mate**   **Cube**

The **tapper is** the flat file like surface or a scuffing tool. Use it in a rolling motion from side to side to seat the chalk into the nap of the leather tip after the tip has been scuffed, or simply tap it, on the top, to seat the chalk. Remember to re-chalk again after seating the chalk with the rolling side-to-side motion. Then, blow off the excess. No need to re-roll or tap the tip the second time, as it will not be necessary, to reseat the chalk again. Do this each time after you have reshaped or re-scuffed your tip, to regain the arc.

Tip Tapper

By chalking the second time, you gain better contact and control of the cue ball, eliminating the potential for miscuing. The general rule, a habit with the Pros, is to chalk each time you come to the table. As Ewa Mataya Laurance states in her book, "The Complete Idiot's Guide to Pool and Billiards," page 46, "you should chalk when you come to the table not when you leave. If you chalk when you leave and then re-chalk when you come to the table, you will cake the chalk and cause the cue tip to glide off the cue ball instead of griping it." (Check out her book for more good advice on chalk.) You do not want that to happen so do not over chalk. You need a light coating of chalk on the leather tip in order to create friction when you strike the cue ball. So less is best. This gives you the control you need to spin, draw and control your game. You will be amazed how much chalk will remain after each shot. It really is not necessary to "over" chalk after every shot, but it is better to be safe than sorry. I know the professional players chalk after ever shot so not to miscue. You want to be sure the tip is covered on the entire crown of the tip.

It is important that the chalk is loose and not overly done on the edges. A smooth layer all over the top of the tip is best. Many players get in a bad habit of drilling the chalk cube. Meaning that they put the

7

tip into the center of the chalk and turn the tip like they were drilling a well. It is better to take the chalk, holding the cue still and stroke the tip side to side rotating the tip until you have an even coverage on the entire crown of the tip. If you just replaced the tip or have just scuffed it to raise the nap of the leather, then I recommend to chalk, seat the chalk and re-chalk the second time evenly, but not seating it the second time. Remove excess chalk by blowing it off or hitting the shaft lightly against the palm of your hand. Do not do this over the table felt.

NOTE: ABOUT A FRESH CUBE OF CHALK

There is a light coating on the chalk surface, just like there is a coating on the cue tip. You will note that only the very center of the chalk cube is actually accessible to soft chalk when the cube is new. The rest of the chalk is coated on the surface. This is done to allow the shelf life of chalk to last longer. Chalk has a tendency to absorb moisture. Therefore, before using a cube of chalk, either sand off the coating or use a knife to scrape off the coating. This will make the entire cube of chalk available to chalking your tip and you will not get into the drilling habit. Use the entire cube to stroke the cue tip from side to side. Too many players think the soft part of the chalk, the bullet area in the center, is the only area to chalk the cue tip and that is why the drilling technique is around. They only use the center of the chalk.

Another thing to keep in mind is, if chalk sits around too long and is not used, it does absorb moisture and when used, it will crumble. Chalk should be dry and soft, powdery when applied. If it crumbles, it is time to get a fresh piece of chalk.

As novice, we sometimes tend to over chalk causing other problems such as, glancing off the cue ball, or getting excess chalk on your bridge hand, ferrule and shaft. Eventually, this will affect your stroke and will also stain your shaft by imbedding the chalk into it. This can be worse than not chalking enough. Either way, too much chalk will cause problems and not enough chalk can cause miscues. Scuffing will most likely be needed when you chalk frequently. The chalk will get a glazed shiny appearance. If it is smooth, then it is time to scuff. This will help to hold the chalk on the tip. Knowing when to chalk, why to chalk and how to chalk, comes with experience.

There are many tools on the market to choose from.

The important thing is to find the ones that you are comfortable using. Here are just a few of the many that are available.

Joe Porper has many tools available for tip and cue maintenance

PrikStik – like the tip pik and Magnum 44, the Prik Stik will scuff your tip.

Porcupine Shaper – This tool will put tiny holes in the surface of your cue tip just like the tip pik does. Just push your tip into the tool and it opens the porosity of the leather to allow chalk to adhere.

Tip Burnisher - with friction, over your tip, it will draw the leather upward and re-shape, the mushroomed tip, to its original shape.

Cut-Rite Cue Tip Shaper/Cutter - Has a metal blade inside that when placed on the cue tip, one end will cut off the excess leather on the side wall and on the other end will shape your tip to the contour of a nickel. Insert your tip and twist to get a perfectly trimmed tip and remove the excess leather.

Cute Rite Tip Shaper /Cutter

Porper Little Shaver – Trims away mushroomed edges. Insert your tip into the tool with the cutting edge facing towards the tip. The round cutter surface will trim the tip straight and in line with the ferrule. Be sure to do this on the rubber mat provided as the blade edge is razor sharp.

Shaper/Tacker - Offers a method to consistently shape your tip as well as a means to scuff and seat the chalk by tapping it into the freshly shaped tip.

- **TipTapper** - rasp like flat piece of metal with a small grip. This is one of my favorite tools. Both Porper and Willard have a good tapper tool. I use this for scuffing the tip and for seating chalk into the tip that has just been scuffed or piked. It is also a great way to shape the tip after a tip has just been replaced. This tool is easily controlled, and a must for all billiard players. You can tap the tip that has just been chalked or I prefer to roll the tapper side to side to seat the chalk. Then, re-chalk and tap your palm or blow off the excess chalk, before your next shot.

- **Tip Pik** – This is another of my favorites and is endorsed by "Mr. Billiards," Tony Long. The tip pik has about 40-50 sharp pin-points. By piking the top of the cue tip, after the coating has been removed, you will make a solid tip, porous and chalk receptive. I use either a straight hard hit to penetrate the leather and open the pores or a hit with a slight twist, to add a little scuff and raise the nap of the leather. This increases the porosity of the tip. When chalked, the chalk adheres to the tip. Chalk to me is like two magnets that have a positive attraction to one another. I recommend after using the Tip Pik and chalking, to use a tapper to seat the chalk into the holes you just piked and then re-chalk or even take the barrel of the Tip Pik and roll the chalk into the pores you provided by piking the tip. The positive ionization occurs when the chalk particles attract and cling to one another, the second chalking, adheres well, giving you a great chalked tip. Again, remove the excess chalk by taping your palm with the cue shaft or blowing over the tip.

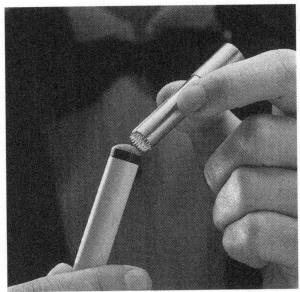

Tip Pik

Here is a good guide for "Cue Stick Grooming and Maintenance." This information provided by Billiards Express, maker of the Tip Pik.

Tip Maintenance

"Your major concern, regarding the tip, should be how well it maintains its shape and holds chalk. The tip should never be smooth or chalk deficient.

1. The tip should be shaped within a dime radius. A gauge is available with most tools.
2. If the tip is not within dime radius, then place a tip shaper tool on the floor with the bowl side upwards.
3. Turn the cue upside down placing the tip of the cue into the shaper bowl.
4. Rotate the cue while pivoting the cue back and forth. Be careful not to over sand and wear the tip down too quickly. Remember, you are not sanding down the tip, simply shaping it.
5. Use a Tip Pik, Tapper or Scuffer on the leather tip to roughen or create deep perforations for maximum chalk retention and better ball control.
6. Apply a small amount of wax to the outside of the tip and burnish. This helps prevent the tip from mushrooming and will sharpen your sights in relation to the cue tip and the ball.

Shaft Maintenance

1. Using No. 600 wet/dry sandpaper, white scotch pad or No. 0000 steel wool, clean the shaft from the ferrule, down to 10-15 inches.
2. Using a piece of brown paper bag, undyed leather, or even a 20 dollar bill, burnish the shaft until it becomes hot to the touch. This gives the shaft a polished look and feel, enabling the shaft to slide smoothly through your fingers.

3. Another option would be to apply a small amount of conditioner to the shaft.

Additional Maintenance

1. To clean and polish the ferrule, use a Pearl Drop Tooth Polish with a dampened cotton cloth and twist the ferrule back and forth.
2. Adding a drop of silicone, shaft treatment of graphite to the joint pin will reduce friction causing the shaft to work smoothly and tighten better.
3. Never apply water to any part of the cue stick."

-The Magnum 44 Tip Scuffer – similar to the Tip Pik, and the Prik Stik, the Magnum 44 is an excellent tool for on the road. Carry it on your key chain with you and you will always have a tool ready for piking and scuffing your tip for re-chalking. The Magnum 44 has multiple edges that you gently use to scuff the surface of your tip. Using the barrel of the 44 you can then imbed the chalk into the naps of the leather and be ready to play.

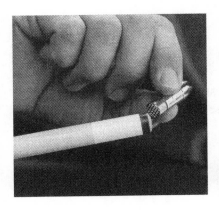

-The Trutip - Another tool like the Porper Cue Rite Tip Shaper. Cuts the tip to a rounded shape each time you insert your tip and turn the tip inside.

-Ulti-Mate - This tool allows you to shape the tip, actually a four in one tool. It burnishes the sides of the tip, and scuffs the tip. It also has sanding capabilities for smoothing the edges of the tip and assisting in its shaping ability.

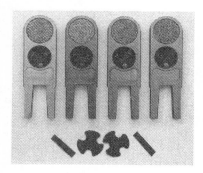

-Willard Shaper - An excellent tool for rounding your tip and creating that arc or curve with the same contour of an American Nickel. Comes with the built in gauge.

-The Cue Cube - Another tip shaper, Scuffs on one side and shapes on the other side. One side of the cube has a greater concaved side than the other which aids in shaping the tip and helps to gain the curved arc that is required for consistent play.

There are many styles of shapers, piks, and scuffers. Pick the ones you feel most comfortable at using and use them faithfully when playing. You will find these tools at the pool halls, billiard stores, on the internet sites that I have listed in the Directory, as well as others, or by subscribing to catalog companies like "Mueller Recreational Products" at www.poolndarts.com or "Saunier-Wilhem Company," at www.swcbilliards.com, to mention two. These are excellent sources for your billiard supplies. Especially, if you live in a market where there is no access to a billiard store or pool hall.

Keep in mind that the tools I speak of are the basic tools required to do a good job of maintaining your tip or even putting the finishing touches on a newly replaced tip. There are more sophisticated pieces of equipment, which cost a few more dollars. They can ease the task that we are performing manually. The basis for this guide is to teach you the basic laymen's method of maintaining a cue tip. Once you have learned the technique with basic equipment and decide you want to invest in more expensive equipment, then, by all means do so. You might even end up doing your friend's cues to recover your equipment cost. Again, manufacturers like Messrs. Porper and Willard make some fine tools for this procedure.

Since we have discussed many of the tools for properly tipping the cue, I would like to present to you Willard's guide to having a properly shaped cue tip. Patricia Sheldon, Willard's daughter has given us this guide to use. It clearly details what shape a properly tipped cue should have, the impact on the cue ball and shows how to test the contour of your arc. This is a good reason to own one of Willard's gauged tools.

You cannot get a precision shaped tip with a hand file or by eye.

With an improperly shaped tip

You aim here...

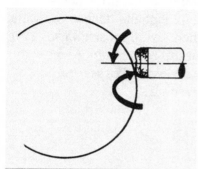

but your tip hits here...

With a Willard's precision shaped

tip you aim and hit here....

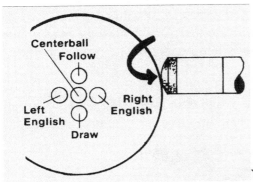

Your tip flattens slightly

when it hits...

The carbide grit shaper is made to the radius
you choose for a precision shaped tip every time.

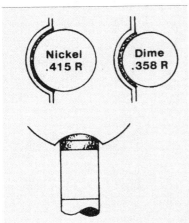

The gauge shows you when is

properly shaped...

Clamping Methods

We have talked about some of the tools needed to maintain a tip. Now, let us add a few comments about the clamps and various methods of holding a tip on the ferrule, while it is drying. I mention these tools briefly only to indicate there are several ways to secure the tip. We will go more in detail when I describe the procedures in Chapter IV.

1. **Plastic clamp** - A "Y" shaped plastic frame, looks like a sling shot, with a rubber band, and a hold clamp to retain the tip, until dry.

1. A. **Plastic Pocket Pal Tip Clamp by Porper** - clamp is in a "U" shape, which covers the tip and aligns against the shaft and is secured with an "O" ring while the tip dries.

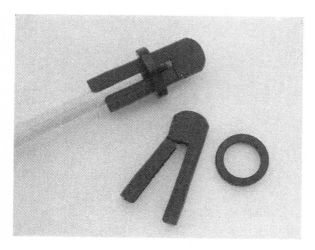

1. B. Tip Clamp by Joe Porper provides the ability to reapply a tip when you are at an event or tournament and you need it at a moment's notice. A compression technique that is rather unique and effective.

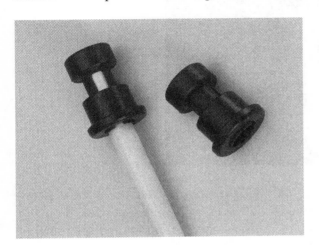

Items 1, 1A, and 1B, in my opinion, are better choices than the metal clamp, for securing the tip. I prefer to use plastic over metal, if I must choose between the two, as each have a risk factor, but the potential for damaging the shaft is greater with the metal than the plastic. No matter which clamp you choose you must be careful not to mare or damage the shaft.

2. The metal clamp and metal connector to hold the clamp. (**Caution -** if using this type of clamp, or any type of clamp, for that matter, remember that the side edges are narrow and can gauge your cue's shaft if clamped too tightly.) It is a good idea to wrap the shaft with a thin rag or paper towel before putting on the clamp and connector. This will help protect your shaft from scaring and creating dents, that must then be sanded, to be removed.

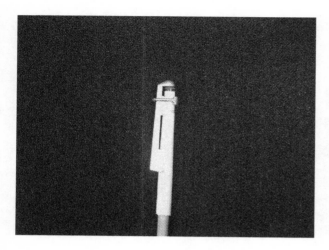

If you are using a good glue or gel, pressure is required to the **center of the tip** during set up but excessive pressure is not needed. You need only a certain amount of tension, to hold the tip in place, until the set up process is completed.

IT IS VERY IMPORTANT THAT YOU DEVELOP A PRACTICE OF BEING CAREFUL WHEN USING THE TOOLS SO AS NOT TO DAMAGE YOUR CUE IN ANY FASHION. TAKE YOUR TIME! DO IT RIGHT AND PROTECT WHERE POSSIBLE. USE GOOD JUDGEMENT AND YOU WILL DO A GOOD JOB.

4. **Rubber Band.** Use a wide 1/2" inch by three or four inch long rubber band. This is my favorite choice. It is inexpensive and easy. Properly applied, it provides the pressure/tension to hold the cue tip in place, while it dries. A simple double half hitch, slid onto the cue, about five to six inches below the ferrule, will provide more than enough tension when stretched to the top, to hold the cue tip in place.

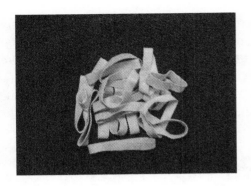

In addition to these tools, you will need some sand paper. 3M makes a 150, 220 and 400 grit paper that will be good for sanding off the tip coatings and pre-sanding the ferrule to remove excess leather. A fine-grained paper is used in post sanding procedures to cleanup after the tip has been installed.

Caution, you should never use a coarse sand paper on your shaft. The finer the paper, the better, as you do not want to mare the finishes. A finer grade of paper is used to clean the shaft. For the Shaft, use a 2400 to 3500 grit or higher, if you can find it. Consider purchasing **Nick's Edge, Cue Slicker, the Q-Wiz** or just a fine untreated piece of **Suede Leather** for cleaning and burnishing the shaft of residues, hand- powder, cue silks and chalk buildups. **McMagic,** by McDermott, are the larger size sheets of very fine papers for cleaning the shaft, comparable to Nick's Edge. Remember to always wash off the cleaning item to get rid of the excess residues before re-using it again. Failure to clean excess residues can lead to marring and scratching your shaft. Like any cleaning product, you should wash them off. **McMagic, Nick's Edge, Q-Wiz, Cue Slicker or could be known as scrunchies** and the rest of the shaft cleaning items are no exceptions. If you cannot afford any of the above, you can always use a dollar bill or a paper towel as the **burnisher** cloth. Both, surprisingly, will clean off excess residues.

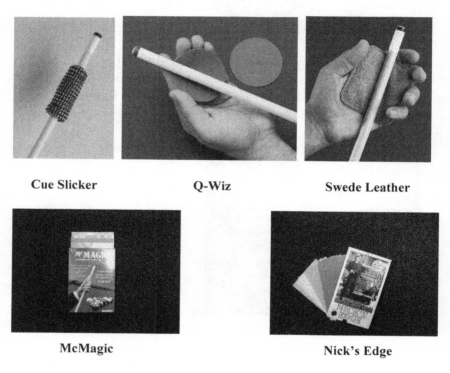

Cue Slicker	Q-Wiz	Swede Leather

McMagic	Nick's Edge

I think a quick note on proper chalking would be in order at this point. When chalking your cue, and this is very important, always hold the tip in a slanting 45 degree angle to the floor, or at an angle that when you chalk, the residues fall to the ground. If your cue is held vertically, the residues will tend to fall onto the ferrule and shaft and your stroking hand, and as you begin to stroke the shaft, for your next shot, you will imbed the chalk into the pores of the shaft and build up will occur. This is what causes your shaft to look grayish or bluish in color. (Depends on color of chalk you are using). The cleaning process would begin all over.

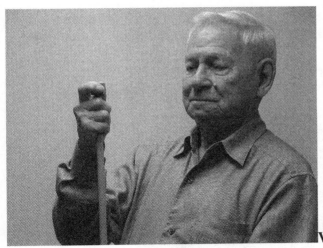

Wrong

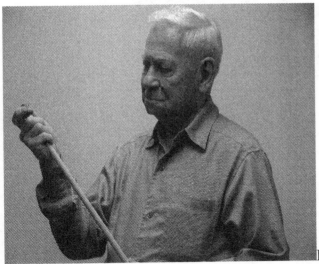

Right

Another hint which is worth noting. Since you want to keep your shaft as clean as possible, remember to carry a soft rag in your cue case. Before you place your shaft into the cue case, with the tip going in first, be sure to wipe off the excess chalk. You can re-chalk before you begin playing again. This will prevent chalk build up on the soft pile liners of your cue case and prevent your shaft from being exposed to chalk rubbing into the pores of the shaft every time you store your cue away. A lot of new players do not realize this is occurring until their once clean shafts, "all of a sudden," have turned blue or gray.

A good bonding **glue,** with "CA" Cyanoacrylate Adhesive, is a major item for consideration. (We will discus various types later)

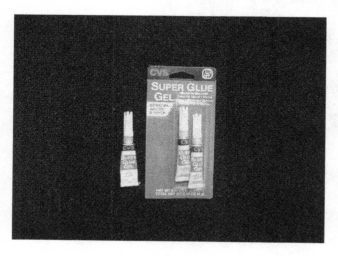

A good shaft cleaner like.

"Shark Oil" or **"Q Clean"** is essential and will help to clean the ferrule after you replace, cut and shape the tip. As a Novice, it will be needed. Depending on the type of cue tip you use, your ferrule may become blue or brown from the dyes in the leather tip. You may also end up with glue on your ferrule that will need to be removed as well. The more tips you replace, the less clean up you will have to do. You will learn by trial and error how to avoid the messes. A good idea is to place a piece of paper around the ferrule and then tape it before you begin maintenance on the tip. I have seen a lot of guys who want to just put tape around the ferrule. Not wise! Remember, tapes have an adhesive bonding material on one side. This leaves tackiness on the ferrule and must be removed. That means more cleaning and sanding. By wrapping the paper first around the ferrule and then taping tightly, you eliminate messy clean ups afterwards.

Now that we have talked about the tools, the shaping, and cleaning, it is time to proceed to the ferrule. I will not go too far in depth on ferrules, as ferrule replacement, in most cases, is a job for a custom cue maker or the manufacturer.

Sharks Oil   **Qclean**

Terry Macioge

CHAPTER II

SIZES OF FERRULES

STYLES AND TYPES OF FERRULES

DANGERS OF OVER CHALKING

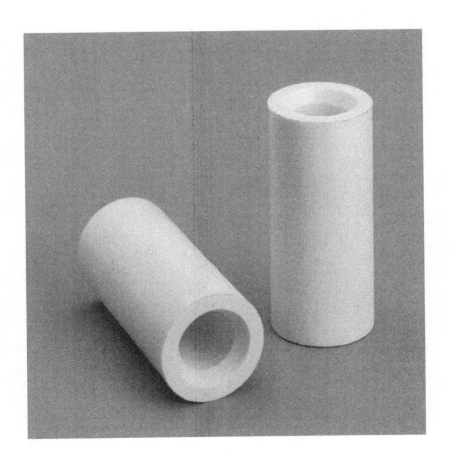

Terry Macioge

Chapter II

The Ferrule

The ferrule is the second part of the cue to take an impact when striking the cue ball. It protects the end of the shaft from splintering, fracturing or cracking. The force from constant impacts can cause a ferrule to eventually fracture. A defective ferrule can cause a loss of resonation from the tip down through the shaft and into the forearm of the cue where you feel it in your grip. There are basically two types of ferrules. One type has a solid capped end or crown, while the second is tubular and open all the way through. The second type permits the tenon portion of the shaft to come through the ferrule and the tip is glued to the top of the tenon and ferrule. Some believe this provides a greater feel and resonation when striking the cue ball. The ferrule is an important part of the cue. It absorbs shock from each hit of the cue ball. When it becomes damaged, or chipped it needs to be replaced. Because of the many types of ferrules on the market and on cues produced by various manufacturers, it is highly recommended that you not attempt to replace your own ferrule, unless you really do not care if you damage the cue. Removing a ferrule manually is not an easy task. If, you have an old cue, that you want to practice on, by all means, go ahead. There are several things you would need to know in order to replace a ferrule the first time by yourself. This really is a job for those who are familiar with all the types of ferrules and have the experience, equipment and knowledge. It is not an easy task to accomplish.

First, you need to know what type of ferrule was used on your shaft. There are different ferrules used on different model cues by different manufacturers. Is it a screw on ferrule, one that has threads inside the ferrule, like those made by McDermott, but takes a regular leather tip?

Screw on Ferrule

Or, could it be a regular ferrule that requires a screw in tip?

Screw in Tip

Is it a push on ferrule with an opening for the tenon of the shaft to come through?

Push On Ferrule

A push on or thread ferrule with a solid crown capped end ferrule?

Capped Ferrule

There is another ferrule that is the push on ferrule with a tip already attached. This is used only on inexpensive cues and is not considered a quality ferrule.

Push on Ferrule and Tip

Sizes

What size is the ferrule, 12mm, 13mm, 14mm (most common sizes) on Pocket Billiard cues that are 57" – 58"etc., with 13mm being the most common of these. Ferrules are 1/2", 3/4", 1", 1&1/4" in length? There are many factors to consider when replacing a ferrule.

Styles and Types of Ferrules

What is the ferrule made of? Do you know what the composition is? Ferrules come in all kinds of materials.

Is it an **Aegis** ferrule?

Maybe it is a **PVC / ABS** ferrule?

Or even a **Fiber** ferrule with cotton texture?

A **Mammoth Ferrule** made from linen based thermoset phenolic resin, which could be a plain ferrule with openings on both ends. Maybe it is one that is capped, or solid on one end.

Is it **Ivory**? The preferred ferrule of most but not affordable to most.

Or, possibly even a ferrule made of **Brass**?

One final type of ferrule is the **Slip on Tip/Ferrule**.

As you can see there are many types of ferrules and knowing what you have is important. The **Aegis ferrule** is most commonly accepted as the replacement for the **Ivory ferrule** used by most custom cue makers. The **PVC ferrule** is constructed of a softer material and provides a good resonation for the player. The feel of each hit is important to the control of your game. If you are a hard hitter, the **Mammoth ferrule** will provide a medium hard hit. Companies like McDermott and Schmelke, JPechauer to name a few, usually produce their own ferrules in house. The **"CT" ferrule** or what I call the cotton textured ferrule, has linen fibers, which add to that terrific feel when you strike a ball. They give that resilience and absorbance of shock that occurs when striking the cue ball. They are pure white and easily distinguished from the **Aegis or PVC** ferrules, which are more off white, cream color or tan in tone. The better the resonation, the better the feel, the better you take control of your game. Although the Aegis is an excellent ferrule, and is considered the substitute for the Ivory ferrule, I prefer the "CT" give of the linen fibers, absorbing the shock of the impact, when you strike the cue ball. To me, it is like driving a car with good shocks, absorbing the bumps. They provide a much better ride. That is what any good ferrule should do. Absorb the impact and provide a good feel down through the cue.

What type of ferrule should you have? That depends on the type of cue you have and the value of the cue. An inexpensive cue would not benefit by putting an Ivory ferrule on it, nor would an expensive cue like a Szamboti, Balabushka or one custom made by Mike Capone, benefit or help your game if you put a screw on tip into a screwed type ferrule. A custom cue maker would shutter if you put a screw on tip on their finely crafted cues. Here is a point to keep in mind. With ferrules that take a screw on tip, you will find that the tip will have a tendency to loosen, with each hit of the cue ball. You might have to buy a lock tight product to prevent the tip from coming unscrewed or get innovative and put a piece of paper on the screw before tightening it down. You would tend to find this type of ferrule on an inexpensive cue. Vibrations from hitting or stroking the cue ball, tend to loosen the screw in tips and will cause the shaft to make a sound with the hit as it loosens. It sounds like a piece of bamboo that has been split and you hit it on the side, A "PING" sound occurs. A broken or cracked shaft, a defective inner core that is cracked, from the manufacturer possibly turning the shaft down to fast, causing the inner core to overheat, or a fractured tenon, will cause the same cracked or broken shaft sounds.

A **Mammoth ferrule** is a good ferrule for a novice player, the beginner who has a tendency to hit the ball hard and has yet to learn the game of finesse. It is an extremely durable ferrule that takes a lot of punishment and is easy to clean because of its hard phenolic resin construction.

The **PVC ferrule** is made of a softer material and will provide a better softer feel with each hit. Good for the finesse player who likes to control the play and uses a lot of soft placement shots.

An **Ivory tip** is usually found on better quality cues and collector cues. It can be special ordered through most manufacturers. A 1" Ivory ferrule will run you about $70-75 to have put on. The ferrule itself runs anywhere from $30-50 depending on where you purchase it. Ivory will age and fracture the same as other ferrules. Ivory has a good resistance to stain but is susceptible to weather and temperature changes and because of expansion and contraction, it absorbs moisture and is susceptible to fractures. As a Novice, it is a good policy to use the "House Cue" for breaking and save your cue for playing the game. Most custom cue makers will likely disagree with me on this and say if the cue is constructed properly, there is no problem breaking with a good made cue. Plus you are breaking with the cue that fits you and your game. I would agree.

Since most of us will never have the luxury of playing with a good custom made cue, I hold by my statement to use the house cue to break with and save your cue for playing the game. If you could afford to own one classic Pontiac GTO or 57 Chevy, etc. you would not drive it thru rain, snow or mud and abuse it. Likewise, if you can only afford to own one cue, why abuse it if you do not have to.

Brass ferrules are usually found in European markets where billiards and snooker are played more often and a short brass ferrule is used. Some inexpensive cues can be found to have brass ferrules but are more for trim and decorative purposes than for producing a quality cue.

Dangers of Over Chalking a Cue

Beginners have a tendency to over chalk and chalk improperly, getting excessive chalk residue on the tip, ferrule and shaft and then rubbing it into the ferrule and shaft with each stroke, causing the dark blue/green /gray looking stains. (Depending on color of chalk you use.) This build up causes the shaft to become tacky/sticky and does not allow for a smooth stroking motion.

There are steps to eliminate this if it occurs and good products available for cleaning your shaft. One thing is for sure, if you want to play a controlled game, you need a clean shaft. Many players do not realize it, but **Nicotine** from cigarette smoke is one ingredient that can really cause havoc on a cue shaft. If you play in a lot of bar areas or pool halls with heavy smoking conditions, the nicotine in the air gets so thick at times, that it is hard to see. This gets on your shafts and then when you over chalk or better yet, improperly chalk getting the chalk on the shaft, it mixes with the nicotine and gets real sticky. Remember to chalk, holding the cue at a 45° angle, to the floor. Do not chalk with the tip in an upright vertical position. This will allow the excess chalk to fall to the floor and not on your ferrule, shaft or stroking hand. Use a good shaft cleaner, "Shark Oil", "Nicks Edge", McMagic, Q-wiz or a good leather cleaning burnishing pad, just to mention a few of the products, and stroke in one direction only to remove excess residues. Holding the shaft with the tip of your cue facing the floor, stroke from the connector joint, towards the tip. Repeat the process going back to the connecting joint and continue until the shaft is smooth and free of all elements. **DO NOT** rub the shaft backwards and forwards, as you will gather the residues, possibly scratching or marring the shaft and imbed the residues into the pores of the wood. Stroke one direction and let the residues go off the end of the shaft, onto the ground.

Here is good tip. The fewer things you put on your shaft, the cleaner it will remain, and the better the glide will be, for your stroke. I see beginners who want to do it all. They put Cue Silk on the shaft, something they should never do. If you use this product, you should only put a drop or two, at the most, on the three bridge fingers, used to hold your cue. This gives a smooth stroke with out resistance on the fingers. Some novice put an ungodly amount of chalk on their hands, to keep them dry. You would think they were gymnast about to mount the horse or uneven parallel bars. If you want to rub all this into the shaft of your cue, go ahead, but I would suggest the glove over additive products, and better yet, why not just take a piece of 6"X6" sweatshirt material and rub it between your hands briskly before starting to shoot. This will dry the oils in your hands and remove the perspiration. Then, take a piece of Nick's Edge, and lightly wrap it around your shaft, give it a few good strokes to make sure there are no residues on your shaft, check your glide and you should be ready to play. If your hands perspire, use the sweatshirt material frequently rubbing until you can feel the heat or dryness. I am a firm believer that the less you put on your shaft, the better control you are going to have, the better sliding motion as your cue glides through your fingers, and the less you will have to worry about cleaning residues off your shaft.

Now, let us talk about the replacement of the ferrule. Once you know what type of ferrule is on your cue, whether it is a push on ferrule or a screw on type ferrule, keep in mind, manufacturers still put glue on the tenon when applying the ferrule and consequently, if you do not know what type ferrule you have, and try to remove it, you could fracture, crack and damage the tenon that the ferrule is glued to. This would then mean hiring a custom cue maker to drill and replace the tenon with a special machine or create a new tenon by cutting and shortening your cue. Over the years, I have seen ferrules that have had clamps applied to them, vice grips, channel locks and other types of tools, in an attempt to remove the ferrule. They latch on and twist or pull to get it off and end up cracking of breaking off the tenon. Removing the ferrule really is an art and takes someone with some experience and knowledge, to do it. I would recommend, if you have a fractured, chipped or damaged ferrule that you want to replace, you seek the assistance of someone in the industry who knows what to do. This would be the manufacturer or a custom cue-maker who made your cue. They are equipped to repair your cues. You may also turn to sources like "Mueller Recreational Products" who offer a full range of cue repairs or possibly you have a good cue maker or trained individual, at a local billiard parlor capable of handling the task.

Mueller's cue repair professionals use state-of-the-art equipment for the best possible results.

Or, check your local directories for those in your area who might do cue stick repair service. There are machines and tools you can purchase for repairing the shaft if you are adventurous and talented craftsman. You could try products produced by Joe Porper, or the Willard cutting and tipping tools, to do your repairs. This depends on how much you want to invest in good equipment to replace a ferrule. Here is the point I need to make here. It would be a waste of your time to tip a cue, if the ferrule is defective.

Assuming that the ferrule is good, let us proceed to discussing the tips, Chapter III, and the many varieties that are available.

Terry Macioge

CHAPTER III

TYPES OF TIPS

SIZES OF TIPS

DENSITIES OF TIPS

BRANDS

CONCLUSION

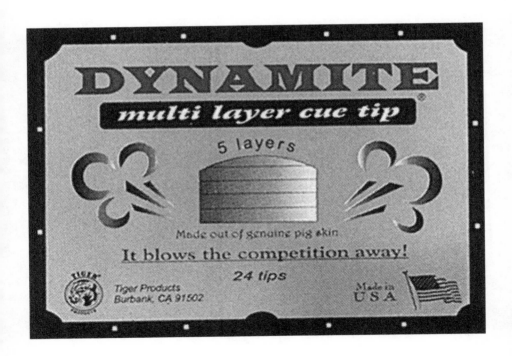

Chapter III

The Tip

The heart of the cue is the tip. Just like the heart pumps blood to all the limbs of your body giving them feeling, so too does the tip of the cue resonate a vibration throughout the cue stick from the tip to the butt of the cue, sending a feeling to your hand with every stroke that you take. To me, and many billiard players, the tip is the most important part of the stick. Every shot begins with the contact that the tip makes on the cue ball. A good contoured tip, with a good arc is more important than the stick that it is on. I have always said, "If you put a good tip, on an inexpensive cue stick, it will perform better, than a poorly shaped tip, on the best custom designed billiard cue."

How important is the tip of the cue? In my opinion, it is the most important part of the cue stick. It is the first thing to touch a cue ball and the major ingredient of controlling your game. The tip of your cue determines the amount of draw, spin and the action you get from striking the cue ball. How it is shaped or curved and prepped for a shot is most important to your controlling your shot and the game.

In 1978 Robert Byrne, in his "Introduction to Byrne's Standard Book of Pool and Billiards," stated "Give Willie Mosconi a broomstick with a good tip and he'll not only make some remarkable shots, he'll sweep the joint out afterward."

Willie Mosconi, was one of the all time great billiard players. According to the stats in the BCA, "Billiards The Official Rules and Records Book", "From 1940 - 1957 he won the World title 15 times." He surely knew the most important part of a cue stick. The game begins at the tip of your cue. A properly shaped tip is essential for a quality game.

45

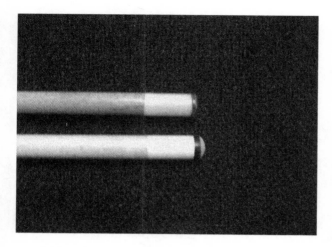

It is important when playing pool, that the arc of the tip remains constant for consistent playing. Many types of tips, which we will discus later, have different characteristics. Some tips, mostly the softer style, will mushroom or flatten out quicker than other tips. This is mostly due to the density of the cue tip. The harder the tip is pressed, the more compressed the leather or synthetic fiber will be, and the denser the tip. The denser the tip is, the stronger the tip. The more impact/compression the tip is capable of handling without mushrooming, the longer the tip will conform to its shape and the better consistency of play you will have. Of course, the player certainly has an effect on the tip as well. If you are a novice and a "banger" type of player, one who thinks that if he hits the ball hard, maybe one will go in, then of course, the tip will most likely mushroom quicker. This happens if it is a softer, less dense, style tip. We will discus the various types of tips in this chapter.

Because tips take a tremendous impact each time you strike a billiard cue ball or break a rack, the pressure of the impact, over the course of time, will tend to flatten the tip. This will affect your level of play. Consistency is very important so that you get the same controlled shot each time. It affects the spin and the draw and how you play each shot. So how do you know if you have the correct shape on your tip? What do you use as a guide for the proper tip? Well depending on where you go and who you talk with, you might get a different answer to this question each time you ask someone. Some players will say,

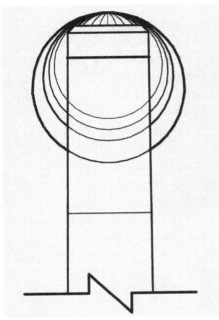

use the side of a quarter, others will say use a nickel, and again someone else might say use a dime. In any event, I feel they are all right. The fact of the matter is, if you take any American coin, lay one on top of the other starting with the largest coin in your pocket, probably the quarter, which has about 1" inch diameter, stack them from the largest to the smallest, a dime, with about 3/4" diameter, you will find the arc or curve of all the coins have a very comparable curve within the width of a 12mm or 13mm tip. By looking at the diagram drawn above, you will get the picture, as I endeavor to explain this.

Beginning with the inner circle, and moving outward. A dime, penny, nickel and quarter

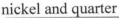

So there is some agreement here, and so we may come to some common analogy, for the benefit of the novice pool player, let us agree that the word arc will mean curve, as described by Webster's Dictionary. The arc and the curve that we are talking about, on each of these coins, is the distance around the common curve of each coin that matches the same distance covered by the width of a 12 or 13mm cue tip. This is the only area of the coin we are talking about. Webster's dictionary, defines an arc as, "a part of the curved line as in a circle." Not to dispute those mathematicians and physicist who would challenge by saying, if the width or the diameter of a coin is greater, then, the arc will be different, with each coin. We agree. What we are talking about is a small segment of the curve, in the 360 degrees, of the coin. That segment represents the width, of the size of a tip, about ½ inch, a very small piece of the curve or arc where little change has taken place and all the coins are constant at this distance. We are talking about comparing the arc of the coins to the arc of the tip. Merely, making a visible comparison and not a micrometer of measurement. Hopefully, we can disburse with any lengthy debates here. Remember we are only trying to determine if the arc, or curve of the tip needs to be reshaped.

Conclusion: assuming that the curves are constant, at that center point, of each arc, which they are, and in alignment with the tip, using any coin, a quarter, nickel, penny or dime, whatever you might have handy in your pocket, you will have a good "guide" for comparing the curve (arc) you need to maintain on your tip, with the curve on any coin. Having the two curves match consistently will provide for consistent play. Placing any U.S. coin, on the side of the ferrule, as shown below, will provide you with this conclusive evidence. You can also purchase tools, like the Willard shaper or Willard tapper that has a built in gauge on their side, the size of a nickel, to give you a guide for whether or not you have the proper shape on your tip. I hope this does not confuse anyone and that you accept it only as a guide to determining if your tip has mushroomed and needs to be reshaped.

 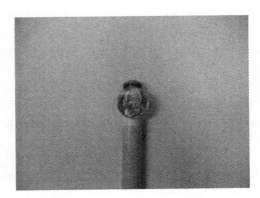

Nickel Arc

Here is what to do. Turn the coin upright as if it were standing on its edge and place it against the side of your cue tip, flat against your ferrule. The top of the coin should line up with the top of the tip of the cue. If they both have the same curve or arc, you are ready to scuff and chalk and continue to play. If not, take your shaper and refine until the tip matches the coin's arc. This is where consistency comes into play. **When there is insufficient tip remaining to get a full arc to match the curvature of the coin, then it is time to replace the tip.** You should not have to reshape the tip after each shot. I once had a young novice player, who was a good customer of mine. He took me to heart and he wanted to be sure, he was playing a consistent game, so after every shot, instead of chalking or scuffing, he would reshape his tip. Obviously, he was coming in frequently to have new tips put on his cue. When I asked how many hours of play he was putting in each week, he said about three days a week about three to four hours a day. His tip should have lasted months, but he took what I said about shaping to heart. Please, if you have an arc, just chalk and continue to play. If you have totally lost the curve, then follow the steps to reshape. How do you know if you have enough leather tip left to get the proper arc? I will explain that shortly.

How to Know When to Replace the Tip

Earlier we talked about when should you replace your tip? Now that we know a little about the tools needed to maintain a tip and what they are used for, and how to shape a tip and using a coin to determine the proper arc of the tip, **we can also use a coin to measure the tip thickness and determine if it needs replaced.**

We established the fact that a good tip will have a constant arc that will match a coin's arc, when turned upright, on its side. Now, if we take a nickel, considering its thickness and turned on its side, place it against the top of the ferrule, in a horizontal position (at 90 degrees to the shaft), and if the tip has been worn down to the thickness of about a nickel, you will not have enough leather tip left to be able to properly reshape the tip any further. It is time to replace the tip.

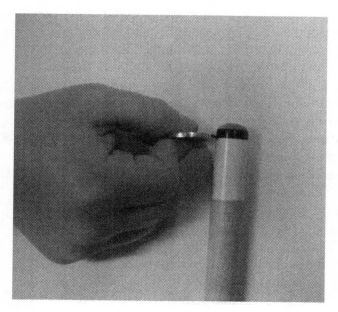

Types of Tips

Tips are made of various types of animal hides; cow hide, calf hide, water buffalo hide, boars hide and pig skin to name a few. The leather is pressed to give it its shape and texture. Some tips are pressed, once, some twice and others even three times. Each time a tip is pressed the degree of hardness increases as the density increases. You are pressing more leather into a smaller compact space. The harder you press the greater the density and the longer the tip will hold its form when properly shaped. There are many types of tips on the market made by various manufactures. I will list and describe a few for you so that you know some of the differences. Not all of them will be mentioned and only through trial and error and changing your tip and shooting, will you come to realize which tip is best for you and your quality of game.

Sizes

Tips come in different sizes. They can range from 7mm to 14 mm for the most part. Snooker and Carom players tend to use a very small, finely, shaped tip, which is usually a 7, 8, or 9mm tip. Snooker is usually the game of preference for most European billiard players. In America, "pocket billiard" games usually are comprised of 8-Ball, 9-Ball, Straight and One Pocket and the cues usually have tips ranging from 12mm to 14mm with 13mm being the most common tip. The 14mm tip, being larger in size, is usually found on break cues. Commonly called the house cue. This gives you the surface advantage of the greatest contact with the cue ball when breaking the rack of balls. A good custom cue maker would say that as a player you should not change the cue to make your break but instead use the same size shaft as you have on your playing stick. In other words, if you play with a Meucci, usually a 12 to 12-1/2 mm tapered shaft or a Helmstetter, J Pechaur, McDermott, Schmelke or other cues, usually 13mm shafts, then do not use a 14 mm stick to break. Do not change your stroke just to break a rack of balls. A good cue should fit your hand and if you are comfortable playing with 12mm then break with a 12mm stick. If you are comfortable playing with a 13mm cue, then break with a 13mm cue and not a 14mm cue.

It is important that you know what size tip you have on your cue. You should always replace your tip with the same size and never, for example, put a 12mm tip, on a 13mm ferrule or a 13mm on a 12 mm ferrule. Tips may vary from size to size in a box, of one-size cue tips. It is best if you can buy individual tips that you know you have sized with your ferrule surface to know that you will get the best fit. It is like buying a pair of shoes, if the fit is right, the results will be a comfortable pair of walking shoes. If the tip does not fit, the feel on the stick will not be the best. No matter if you buy an entire box of one-size tips, you should select the ones that best fit the ferrule on your cue. There will be variances in sizes in the box. Place each on the ferrule before gluing to be sure of the best fit. Because of the way tips are compressed, shapes will not always be consistent, even in an entire box of one-size. A certain amount of shaping, cutting and preparing for play, will be required, for every tip.

Tips come in different colors. Leathers are dyed. Some can be blue, some brown, or tan and some black and other combinations. Color is not important unless you are trying to blend it to match your inlays and colorful wraps and wood tones of your cue. That would indicate that you are more concerned about looks than playability. The same applies to the ferrules when people try to match the ferrules. But, if you can get it to match and still get a game quality tip, then by all means go for it. In other words, color really does not matter. It is control and playability that counts. Tips vary from soft densities to extra hard so you will need to use many styles before you find the one that suits your present game. As Ewa Mataya Laurance points out in "The Complete Idiot's Guide to Pool and Billiards," p.82, she recommends that "you begin playing with a soft to medium-soft tip which will give you the ability to have a good spin on the ball." "When you develop a good stroke you will reach a point where you are putting too much spin on the ball and that will be the time to increase the hardness of your tip, most likely to a medium density tip. This will give you control of your spin again and allow you to maintain the good stroke you have developed."

Densities of Tips

Different tips have different densities and range from soft to hard and some extra hard. This factor in itself is probably the most characteristic feature of a tip. Changing the degree of softness to medium density to a very firm hard tip will change the playability of the cue. When you alter the tip or change its density you change the controllability of the tip. The softer the tip, the more likely the tip will mushroom. For the novice, mushrooming is when the tip tends to flatten out with each hit of the cue ball. The tip being soft flattens out and rolls over the sides of the ferrule. Thus, it gives the shape and look of a mushroom. A soft tip will need to be maintained more and require that you shape it frequently to keep the arc and consistent playability. Some players think that a softer tip allows a greater contact with the cue ball and consequently better control and action with each stroke. Some believe the softer the tip, the greater amount of English, spin that can be gained on contact. The soft cue tips require frequent shaping to maintain the shape but are easier to scuff, and easier to chalk. The problem with a soft tip is that it tends to require more shaping, more often. Therefore, it will need to be replaced more frequently. On the reverse, a harder, heavier density tip will require less shaping and will not flatten or mushroom as easily. It will tend to hold its shape longer giving you a more or longer consistency of play. The harder tip will require more scuffing in order to hold the chalk properly. A good tip pik or tip tapper is helpful when scuffing a hard tip. Or, as Robert Byrne, National Class Billiard Player, and best billiard's instructional author has done, he takes two grades of sand paper and glues them to a block of wood. He finds this technique more useful for scuffing his tips than using the smaller hand tools. You can find Bob's procedure in his book, "Byrne's New Standard Book of Pool and Billiards" on pages 7and 8. You will tend to chalk more with the heavier density tips. Heavy density tips tend to lose their chalk quicker. Once again, I suggest that you pik the tip, chalk it, seat the chalk with your tapper and re-chalk again. This way the chalk will cling or adhere to the chalk that is already imbedded in the leather pik holes and consequently will hold longer. The result will provide for better ball contact and chalk will last longer on the heavier density tips. I have tried to convey this method of chalking to better players who use the medium to heavier density tips and they seem to agree, they get better results, if chalked in this manner. Chalking twice does work. (Incase you did not understand this procedure for medium to heavy density tips, I recommend you re-read the last 3-4 sentences. Again, I remind you that you should always remove the excess chalk from the tip prior to taking your next shot. Tap your cue lightly against the palm of your hand with the tip pointing downward or merely blow across the top of your tip to remove the excess. Your heavier density tips will tend to last longer and will need replaced less frequently. They tend to be more consistent, hold the arc longer and provide for a more controllable contact with the cue ball. These heavier density tips are for the finesse player.

How does one determine the density, of the tip, on his cue? If you do not know what tip the manufacturer used on the cue when you purchased it, or your retailer does not know, especially if you purchased the cue in a regular sports retail store, you can use your thumb nail and apply pressure to the tip. The more your nail sinks into the tip, the softer the tip will be, and the less dense. Barry Szamboti also takes his tips and bits the sides. If he leaves teeth impressions he knows that the tip walls or shoulders will be weak and not good for the impact it will receive, and he rejects those. To me this is good sound reasoning. If the foundation walls collapse, you end up with mushrooming. Most medium to hard density tips will be pressed so hard that your nail or teeth will not make an impression. **"Mueller's Recreational Products" Catalog will show the densities of the tips they sell. Joe Porper also sells a machine that will register the density of tips.**

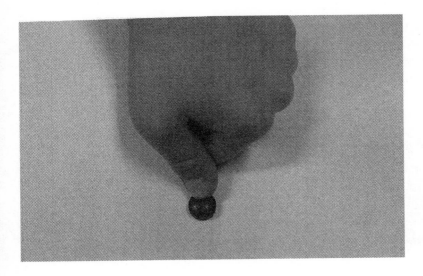

For your convenience, "Mueller's Recreational Products" has provided many of the photographs for the tips used by this author and they have graciously given the densities that these tips have tested. This will help you in determining the densities of the tip you prefer. (Note: the new Tiger Sniper Brand reflects the European Density scale for rating).

Many store clerks will not be familiar with the different types of cues that they sale, let alone the different types of tips, on a cue. If you have a local favorite billiard store, ask to see a variety of tips and test the different brands to determine what level of density you want to try. Be adventurous at first until you find the one that works for you. As your game improves you will most likely find yourself moving from a soft density tip to a medium to heavy density tip. From this point, it is just deciding what brand you favor most.

Here are some of the types of tips that are available for you to choose from.

Some of the most commonly know and used tips are:

(The lower the number, softer the tip, higher the number, the more density to the tip and the harder it will be.)

Elk Master- (Blue) soft leather tip with a density of 60.1

Royal Oak-oak tanned leather with a density of 66.5

Blue Knights- (Blue) **soft** leather tip density of 61.2

Le Pro / Le Professional- (brown) tip of **medium hard** density of 78.2

For the price and quality, this is one of the better oak leather tips available.

Triumph- is another **medium hard** density tip of 76.9

There are others such as:

Silver King - Soft density tip made from specially treated leathers with a rating of 60.3

Chandivert French Tips - they make both **soft** and **hard** tips with a range of different densities.

- **Eureka** - **soft** tips with a density of 64.4. These are vegetable tanned and double pressed finish.

- **Champion** - **medium hard** density of 74.2 vegetable tanned with red or black fiber bottom.

- **Super Royal** – **medium** density of 75.8 Gray fiber-backed leather tip is vegetable tanned and double pressed.

- **Crown** - **hard**, double pressed at a density of 77.1

- **Comprime** – made from thick leather, vegetable tanned and double pressed at density of 78.7

Everest -10 layered laminated pigskin tips, **medium** density of 75.1

This tip shapes like a hard tip, hits like a medium and has control like a soft tip.

Tiger laminated - soft to hard density 11 layered pigskin tips.

The **Soft** 65.3 density are made out of white color cowhide giving you the benefit of a soft tip without the mushrooming. Both the **Medium** 74.5 and **Hard** 81.0 tips are dark brown in color and made with two different types of treated pig skin.

Sniper new by **Tiger-** "Sniper laminated cue tips are made from a boar hide that is tanned the old fashion way, under ground. Treated slowly and without any chemicals, each hide takes up a full year to tan." Based on the European method of determining density, on a scale of 95-100 with 95 being soft, 96, medium, **97 medium hard**, 98 is hard. This tip rates at a **density of 97.**

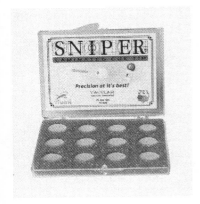

The Stingray - made of 11 layers of cold weather pigskin, **hard** density tip of 83.5

Talisman Pro tips - Holds it shape and never mushrooms, **medium hard**, 77.0 density.

Talisman Water Buffalo -medium hard 76.3 made from high grade buffalo hides. This tip gives you superior ball control and greater consistency. Holds chalk longer and will not mushroom.

The Majestic – Porper's multiple layered tips with low maintenance. Made from split calfskin and bonded with a specially formulated agent. This tip has a **Medium Hard** density of 77.4

Hercules – Adams Ltd. "Over 20 ply Pigskin. This tip contains over 20 layers of chrome vegetable tanned selected Pig-skin. The tip requires very little maintenance to bring out the beauty of the cue control on every shot"

Terry Macioge

H2 – New **by Adams Ltd,** this is a second generation multi dimensional layered tip with about 12 layers. It is a **medium to hard** density tip.

Shooter – **Adams Ltd**. "8 ply water buffalo leather tip. This inexpensive tip will not mushroom and gives a sensitive feel from the tip through the entire cue"

Black Diamond – Adams Ltd. 11 ply water buffalo. "The black diamond is a laminated top grain water buffalo tip. This tip will last 5-6 times longer than standard one piece tips and will not mushroom."

Regal – another fine tip by **Adams Ltd**. "dual pigskin with select water buffalo leather. This tip last 5-6 times longer than the one piece tips without mushrooming."

Terry Macioge

Finally, a new futuristic tip called the

Leather-syn (synthetic tip) - hard density. This tip will hold its shape and will not mushroom. Comes in either the smooth finish or rough finish. Cost about $9 a piece.

The only other type of tip remaining is the screw in tip. Occasionally a cue manufacturer will use a screw in tip on less expensive cues. You might need to wrap the threads with a piece of paper in order to lock it in to prevent it becoming lose while playing.

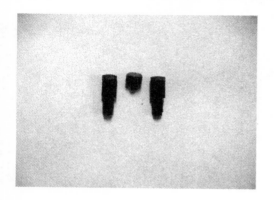

For quick reference - tips summarized

Tip Name	Type	Density	Plys
Elk Master	Soft	60.1	n/a
Royal Oak	Soft	66.5	n/a
Blue Knights	Soft	61.2	n/a
Le Pro	Med. Hard	78.2	n/a
Truimph	Med. Hard	76.9	n/a

Silver King	Soft	60.3	n/a
Chandivert French Tips			
- Eureka	Soft	64.4	n/a
- Champion	Med. Hard	74.2	n/a
- Super Royal	Medium	75.8	n/a
- Crown	Hard	77.1	n/a
- Comprime	Hard	78.7	n/a
- Rocky	Very Hard	82.1	n/a
Sumo	Hard	82.0	n/a
Ram	Soft	64.1	n/a
	Medium	75.1	n/a
Triangle	Hard	81.4	n/a
Dynamite	Med. Hard	77.2	n/a
Wild Boar	Med. Hard	77.8	11
Tsunami	Medium	75.8	12
	Hard	82.4	12
Stratos	Soft	65.8	12
	Medium	75.5	12
	Hard	81.1	12
	Extra Hard	87.3	12
Everest	Medium	75.1	10

Terry Macioge

Tiger	**Soft**	**65.3**	**11**
	Medium	**74.5**	**11**
	Hard	**81.0**	**11**
New Sniper	**Med. Hard**	**97.0**	**10-12**
Stingray	**Hard**	**83.5**	**11**
Talisman Pro	**Med. Hard**	**77.0**	**n/a**
Talisman WB	**Med. Hard**	**76.3**	**n/a**
Majestic	**Med. Hard**	**77.4**	**multi**
Hercules			**23**
H2			**12**
Shooter			**8**
Black Diamond			**11**
Regal			**multi**
Leather syn	**Hard**		**n/a**

One last note about tips, if you are desperate and need a quick fix, you can always put on a **"slip on" tip/ferrule** combo. I hate suggesting you use these tips, but for the cheaper priced cues and those who do not want to replace the existing tip with a good quality tip or pay a person to put on a good tip, this is a quick fix. I would recommend this only on those very inexpensive cues that cost under $20. Cues which are not worth investing in good quality tips. These tips crush quickly, are difficult to shape properly, if at all, and do not provide the contact and feel that you need to play a good quality game. Enough said about slip on tips.

Slip on Tip/Ferrule

Conclusion, there are many styles of tips, in many sizes and different densities, many degrees of softness or hardness, and many cue manufacturers who make their own tips for their products, which are also available, for purchase. The choices are plenty. You just need to find the one that suits your game. There will be as many opinions as to which tip is better or best, but that decision is going to be yours. It is your game and stick that determines how you play.

The prices are as varied as the types that are available. Obviously, when you purchase in quantity or by the box, the prices are less per tip. I would recommend that you purchase individually for a while so that you can try a variety of tips until you find the one that suits you best. Then purchase by the box so you never run out. Some tips like the laminated and layered tips are more expensive and some only come in the larger 14mm size which means you will have to shape the tip and cut it to fit your cue. This will require some tools to make the task easier. As I said before, Porper and Williard are two suppliers who make a range of tools to make your job easier.

Now that we have talked about the various types of tips that are available, the sizes of tips, the density of tips, the color of tips, it's time to find out, how to put the tip on your stick. You have made your tip selection and now you want to put it on.

So, let us go to the last and final chapter of "How to Tip a Pool Cue."

Terry Macioge

CHAPTER IV

TOOLS YOU WILL NEED

THE GLUE

THE PROCESS

THE CLAMPS

THE CLEANUP

Terry Macioge

Chapter IV

"How to Tip A Pool Cue"
"The Laymen's Guide"

Well, hopefully by now, you have learned something about ferrules and tips and now you need to decide what tip is best for your game at this time. You have determined that your tip needs to be replaced and found the tip you want to try and now need to learn how to tip the cue. It is going to be easy. So relax. By the time we get through this chapter, you will be ready to tackle the task. The photos should provide the visual help needed for you to understand how it is done.

We have reviewed the types of tools and equipment needed for tipping the cue. We also talked about the many types of ferrules that are on cues and the examination of the ferrule, prior to replacing the tip. In Chapter III, we reviewed many of the different types of tips that are available for your cue. Finally, we talked about the sizes and densities, of tips, and are ready to put this information to work for us. Let us talk about how to replace the old tip on your cue with a new tip.

What Tools Do We Need?

We need a good cutting implement. A sharp knife or razor blade is a must. I like to use the thinnest cutting tool I can get that is controllable so I do not cut myself. If you own a plastic top sander or one of the better metal rapid top sanders, this is a plus. Top sanders usually use a sand paper that is 300 - 320 grit. The ferrule metal top sander takes a 317 grit paper. You will have to remove the balance of any leather that may remain on the ferrule.

After you have removed as much of the tip, as close to the ferrule, as possible, you want to put the sander to work on the ferrule, to be sure the ferrule is as level and flat, as possible. Place a credit card or a solid flat item, on top of the ferrule. Check to see if it is perfectly flat or if any light might be coming through underneath the card. If you see daylight, then proceed to sanding more, until it is perfectly even.

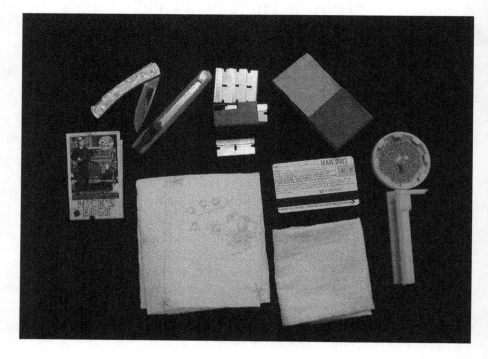

Tools for the Tip Changing

Caution: You do not want to sand the ferrule very much removing the excess leather for fear you will wear the ferrule thin. This is particularly most important on capped end ferrules. If you grind through this end, you will need to change the ferrule, a task you might not be able to accomplish easily. If it is a ferrule with an open end, you will have less concern but should still be cautious in sanding. Take down only as much as is absolutely needed to remove the excess leather and assure that the ferrule is perfectly flat.

Metal - Rapid Cue Top Sander

The Removal Process and Clamps

To start to remove a tip, assuming that it was not knocked off from dropping the cue, and that you have reached the point now where your tip can not be reshaped any more, use a razor blade or a knife, your choice, to remove the majority of the tip as close to the ferrule as possible. I find that I prefer the single edge razor blade with a thick gripping edge on one side and laying the shaft on a flat surface, place the blade as close to the edge of the ferrule as possible and then using a slow rolling back and forth motion of the shaft, while pressing on the blade, I can cut easily through the tip. After removing the majority of the leather tip, you must remove the balance through a sanding process, so that the ferrule is perfectly flat.

Caution: It is a good idea when sanding to place a rag, or hanky around the shaft when you are mounting the sander to the shaft in preparation to smooth the ferrule. This will help protect the shaft from being marred or scratched. You can also cut a small piece of paper and insert it in the mounting clamp so that the metal does not make contact with the shaft.

It is imperative that the top of the ferrule be made as flat and even as possible in order for the replacement tip to adhere. The sander or sand paper, are essential to accomplish this. If you do not own a sanding tool, you can take a sheet of sand paper, place it on a perfectly flat surface and removing the shaft from the cue, rub the top of the ferrule cautiously from side to side and sand off any excess leather. Make sure to keep the shaft always in a vertical position to be sure you are sanding flat. Any curvature on the ferrule will cause the tip to come off after it has been glued. Another method to properly sand the ferrule to remove excess leather would be to take a sanding block, or tack a piece of sand paper to a piece of wood to make a sanding block, and then lay your cue on a flat surface, with the edge of the ferrule in line with the edge it is laid on. Taking the sanding block against both surfaces, to keep the block flat, sand cautiously while holding the shaft firmly against the sanding block, to remove the excess leather.

You will need to choose the method you would like to use to hold the tip in place while the glue is setting.

- You can purchase the plastic "Y" clamp and retaining connector

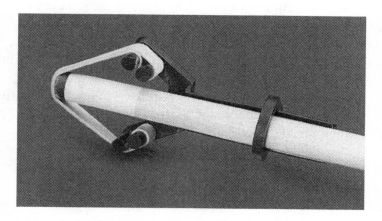

- or, use the metal clamp with the triangular shaped connector

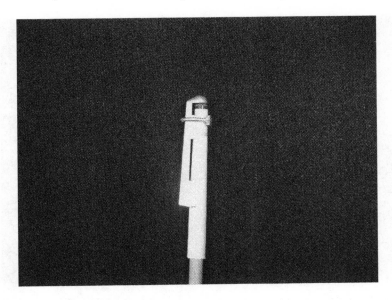

- or, the **Porper Pocket Pal** "U" shaped clamp with an "O" ring

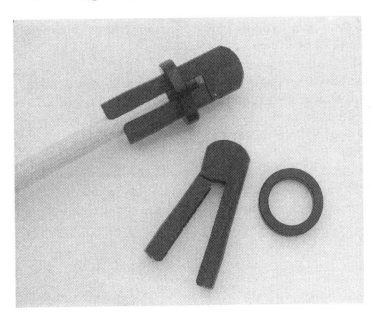

- or use a rubber band.

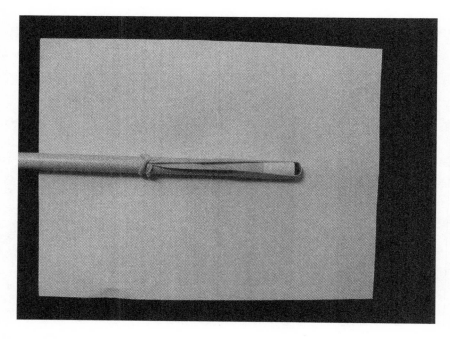

I will explain later how to apply each of these methods. There are others, and you can be inventive if you like.

You can purchase tip repair kits that will include, the grinder, the glue, a clamp, tips and sand paper and more. Just about everything you need to do the job. A kit like this will range in price from about $10-15 dollars.

You should have a 9" cue tip trimmer. A curved, half moon shaped, metal or plastic holder that has a long strip of sand paper inside. This item will curve and shape your tip to give you that perfect arc.

Cue Tip Trimmer

Spare sand paper of different grits will be helpful. A shaper, a tip pik, a tapper can also make your installation easy. If you own a Porper Cut-Rite Tip Cutter, this would be a plus.

| **Shaper** | **Tip Pik** | **Tapper** | **Cut-Rite Tip Cutter** |

The most important item, the Glue.

There are many types of glues on the market, and many say for leather on the packaging. The problem is you need glue that not only holds or bonds leather, but you also need to have a glue that will adhere to wood, plastic and different poly fibers at the same time.

Tweeten's 10 Minute Cement seems to be the choice of most people who replace tips. This glue sets up in 10 minutes and is applied like contact cement. Apply it to both surfaces, let stand for a few minutes and then join the two surfaces together. Clamp the tip to the ferrule and you are done. It is recommended that you allow 24 hours for this cement to fully cure, before shaping the tip and playing. Z-Poxy and

Tiger are two other glues that are acceptable. Bob Byrne likes the Elmer's White Glue. Barry Szamboti uses glue with the same "CA" base ingredient that I like and Mike Capone, like many other custom cue makers, uses the Locktite 454 glue. This is glue of preference for many of the cue makers. Duro Manufacturing Company makes glues with the "CA" base and these are strong, quick bonding glues. Just be sure the glue tube or package states it can be used on multiple materials, such as, wood, plastic, and leather, in order to bond well.

Tweeten's

I have tested and tried many different types of glue on the market and have found one that works well for me. If you have a CVS Pharmacy in your market, they carry glue and gel, in their private label package, which is superior, to other glues that I have used, in the years I have been tipping cues. It is Super Glue, "Gel". "Gel" being the key word here. This item comes packaged two tubes per package for about $1.10 - $1.20. That is a lot of tipping in two tubes. On the reverse side of the package, it will state, "CVS Super Glue Gel is an advanced formula **cyanoacrylate adhesive** which combines the convenience and control of a "Won't run" gel with the fast-bonding properties of Super Glue. I believe the key words here are the ingredient, **cyanoacrylate adhesive. Be sure to get the Red and Black package that says on the front, "Bonds in seconds, Great for Metal, Wood, Glass, Plastic, Rubber, Ceramic and Leather."** That covers all bases. This Gel sets up fast. I mean **FAST.** Let me say that again. **It is FAST setting**. It only takes 10 seconds to dry, as opposed to 10 minutes of Tweetens, to set up. CVS 's Gel will be ready to play in the time it takes you to shape and prep the tip. No need to wait over night or long hours for the curing process before you can begin to play.

If you feel that this fast setting gel will not provide you the time, to set the tip firmly in place, on your first attempt, then you might want to try it with the Tweeten's Cement first. After you have done a few tips, then try the CVS Gel. I feel confident, that you can do it, in ten seconds. It will not take you ten seconds to put a tip on and make sure it is properly aligned.

Assuming that you have removed the excess leather of the old tip from the ferrule and made sure the top of the ferrule is flat and ready to apply a new tip, here is what you would do. Very conservatively, you would apply a pin tip size drop of the gel to the center of the ferrule. "Did you hear that, use a Pin tip amount." It does not take much. In-fact, in this case, less is better. Taking the already prepped tip, a leather tip of your choice, you should have taken a piece of the 3M sandpaper with a grit of 220 - 400 and rubbed off any coating that is on the bottom of the tip. Example: The Le Pro tips are coated. Sanding off the coating on the bottom will allow the gel or glue to adhere better. The smooth coating would prevent the tip from adhering well so it is important that the coating be removed. Then, here is a little trick I learned over the years. **Take a tip pik, or the Porper Porcupine, the item with about 40- 50 sharp points, and**

pik the bottom of the tip. Note, you can use a pin but it takes a lot longer. You will need to push very firmly to make the indentations. You only need to enter the base of the tip slightly so that the glue will have space to enter. Never go deeper than the thickness of a dime. By putting shallow perforations in the bottom, it will allow the Gel or Glue to ooze into the leather and provide a grip like never before. This is the secret that has made my tipping so successful. Only one cue tip out of thousands that I have tipped has ever fallen off. Honestly, had the owner not dropped it on the concrete floor, he would probably still be playing with the same tip today.

If I have a wooden tenon through the ferrule and not a solid capped ferrule, I tend to pik the wood ever so lightly. You do not have to do this, but I do on my own cues. Now, apply a small amount of gel or glue, about the size of a pinpoint, directly in the center of the ferrule. Then, taking the tip, swirl the gel in a circling motion to be sure the entire surface area is completely covered with the gel.

Caution here. This gel sets in ten seconds so this must be done rapidly. The point is you are covering both surfaces by doing this, and bonding the gel into the pores of the wood and the leather at the same time. When this sets, it will set fast, so you must swirl quickly and be sure you have taken out any possible air bubbles. This is not likely to occur with the CVS Gel, although it does present itself with other types of glues. If this occurs, what will happen is it will dry but an air pocket forms between the ferrule top and the tip bottom and when you make your first contact with the cue ball, chances are the tip will pop off.

What I do is hold the tip perfectly in alignment with the ferrule edges, making sure that the tip is perfectly centered or centered as best as can possibly be, and apply a slight pressure for setting. I use the rubber band method, so as not to mare or scratch my shaft. Prior to putting the gel on the ferrule, I affix the rubber band to the shaft of the cue by using a double half hitch method.

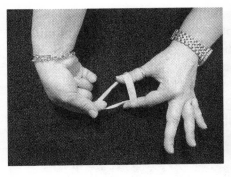

Step 1

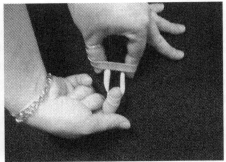

Step 2

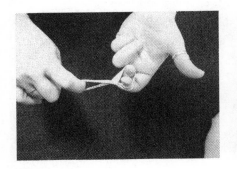

Step 3

Step 4

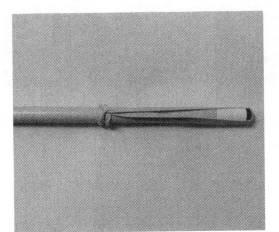

Step 5

Place the rubber band about five to six inches below the tip of the ferrule and pull tightly. If you do not know how to make the double half hitch, then merely take the rubber band and wrap it around the shaft about 5-6" below the top of the ferrule. Pinch one end of the rubber band and open the other like you are threading a needle. Slide the rubber band through the opening and pull tightly. This will make the same knot, as if you made a double half hitch, and slide it over the ferrule.

Be sure to test the stretch limit to be sure it reaches the top of the ferrule easily before you add the glue and tip. Not all rubber bands have the same elasticity. If it does not reach, then move your rubber band closer to the ferrule top and re-tighten. When you have mounted the tip on the ferrule, hold it in place for 10 seconds, and then stretch the rubber band over the tip to hold it under slight pressure for about 10 -15 minutes, assuming that you are using the CVS Gel, or a product with "CA" adhesive base. (Make sure that the tip stays in line with the ferrule edges and make any necessary adjustments quickly.) After that, you can remove the rubber band and begin shaping your newly installed tip. That is all there is to putting the tip on solid.

At this point, the 9" sander is used to shape the tip,

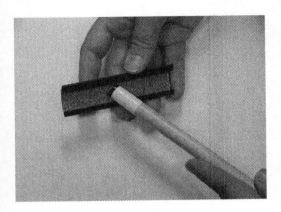

remove the top coating and give it the contour of the American coin as discussed earlier. I use a tip tapper tool in lieu of the sander to form the arc of the tip. I find that the file like tool is very easy to use to shape the tip, remove the coating on the top of the tip and I get better results than if I used the 9" sander. It just happens to be my personal preference. You too might find one tool will work for you better than another. Assemble the shaft to the stock and using the tip tapper, at a 45° angle, to the tip, as you rotate the shaft, with the butt on the floor, strike the tip at a 45° angle and cut the curve of the tip to form the arc.

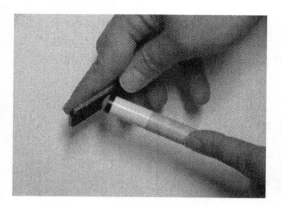

A few good strokes and you will be around the entire tip and ready to pik it. This is equivalent to the cue maker using his lathe to turn the shaft while he puts the leather-cutting tool to the tip to form the curve. As laymen we have to improvise to achieve what the machine accomplishes easily.

Note: It is important that all the coating on the top of the tip be removed. If it is not, then the chalk will not adhere to the tip. It is amazing how many new players are never told this and then they wonder why the chalk will not stay on. After you remove the coating, begin the scuffing and piking process, to raise the nap of the leather, for the chalk to adhere.

Once the shape has been achieved, take Magnum 44 Porper's Prik Stik or a tip pik, whatever sharp edged tool you may have at your disposal, and with very hard and very precise strokes, carefully pik the tip making sure to pik the entire arched surface. Medium to Hard density tips will require more effort to make the naps rise. I make sure my fingers holding the shaft, are about five to six inches below the ferrule. This step can be risky, so be careful if you try this. You MUST hold the cue very firm against your thigh when piking, especially when using the Tip Pik, in order to keep the cue as steady as possible. The pik needles are extremely sharp and will draw blood if you miss your pik stroke and hit a finger. Beginners might want to use the scuffer tool in lieu of the tip pik just to prevent a possible mishap. If you are not scared of the risk, then start with small piks and increase your stroke to get a deeper penetration into the leather tip as you gain stroke confidence. If it is a soft density tip, be sure to use very little pressure, as it will raise the nap of the leather, very easily. If the tip is a Le Pro, a medium to hard density tip, a heavy piking is required to make the perforations on the top of the tip. A hit and twist motion will raise the nap so that you can then begin to apply chalk. Be sure to apply an adequate amount of chalk, as it will be seated, the first time. Be sure to cover the entire arc surface with the piking. At this point, taking the tip tapper, and rolling it from side to side, I imbed the chalk into the perforations created by the tip pik. Or, you can just tap the top of the tip by letting the taper bounce off with each stroke as you push the chalk into the pik holes and nap of the leather. Repeat the chalking process, all the time, holding the shaft with the tip facing in a downward slanted position and not vertical, so as to keep the chalk from falling onto the shaft and ferrule. After the second chalking, I tap the shaft against the palm of my hand or blow off any excess and the tip is ready to use. At this point, to be sure I have a successful gluing, I take my assembled cue and head for the pool table. My test is simple. I use only the cue ball on the table and if I can get 2 1/2 to 3 rails, up and back, like you do when you lag to see who is going to break the opening rack, then I know I have hit the cue ball hard enough to cause the tip to come off, if it was not properly prepared. If you can successfully accomplish getting 2-3 rails without the tip popping off, then you have completed the tipping job well.

I want to take a moment to make a very important point regarding glues or gels. First, you need to find the glue or gel with the characteristics that have been described in the CVS statement or as indicated on Tweeten's Cement. Mike Capone, a custom cue maker, likes the Locktite 454 glue. This is one of the preferred glues by many of the custom cue makers. It sets up and bonds great with super strength. Second, I do not like to use Crazy glue, as it does not seem to hold as well. I'm not talking about the Crazy Gel, but the glue itself. It seems to crystallize rather than remain in a pliable condition like gels do, and they tend to crack or separate from the ferrule and bottom of the tip causing the tip to pop off. Elmer's paper glue, (not the Elmer's White that bonds, ceramic, wood, plastic and paper), other paper glues and shop wood glues by themselves, some contact cements, some epoxy glues and other glues of this nature that do not cover all three component materials, will not work on your leather and wood and various composition ferrules. Finally, **excessive amounts of glues** will definitely not work. I have seen cues where the owners have practically dipped the tip into the glue and the glue ran down the ferrule and shaft and they could not understand why the tip did not hold. **Less is Best.** Please remember, a pin drop, the amount equal to the tip of a pin, is all that is needed, if you are using the CVS gel or even the Tweeten's Cement. You do not need a lot to do a good tip job. The secret is finding a gel with the "CA" compound or checking places like Sears Hardware which carries several glues, and one labeled Super Gel, that have the ability like the CVS Gel, to bond wood, plastic and leather. The key is to find that glue or gel that once applied and cured will hold under the severe impact pressure generated by the tip and its contact with the cue ball.

Caution: Since you are working with a glue or gel, it is a good idea to be prepared for the worse. SAFETY first! I recommend you read the label and know what to do should you accidentally get your fingers stuck together. I hate to admit it, but I have been victim, on many occasions. So please, read the manufacturer's warnings, on the label, before you open your glue (gel). I like to keep a bottle of fingernail polish remover handy as it dissolves glue rapidly and frees the fingers. It contains acetone, which dissolves the cyanoacrylate, to free the fingers.

Now I would like to back track and discuss the use of the other three styles of clamps and another technique, for applying pressure to the tip.

1. Let us assume we have prepped the ferrule and tip and have applied the gel and are ready to put the **metal clamp** and **connector** on to hold the tip in place. Here is a CAUTION.... prior to using the metal clamp, I highly recommend that you wrap a paper towel, or soft cloth, like a hanky, around the shaft to give some degree of protection against any scratching or marring of the shaft. Then, place the tip on, using the same swirling procedure, as described earlier, to smooth out

the pin drop of glue and apply the metal clamp. Here is the second caution. We are macho men and women, right... but as laymen, we think we need to push the clamp connector on and down the shaft, as hard as we can, so as to apply major pressure, to the clamp and thus putting pressure on the newly replaced tip. **This is far from the truth and is exactly what should not be done.** The clamp is merely to apply enough pressure to the center of the tip to hold the tip in place while drying. Very little pressure is required to accomplish this. By exerting excessive pressure you push the sides of the clamp into the shaft creating scratches and dints in the shaft. This will require major sanding to correct the error and you will never forgive yourself for this error. Any dint in the shaft, especially in the first 14 inches of the shaft will definitely affect the feel and stroke of your game. I do not like to put anything on the shaft that is going to scratch or mare it. I prefer the rubber band or nothing at all, a technique my friend Walter uses, that I will describe to you shortly.

All other steps after the tip is dry are the same.

2. The **plastic clamp, "Y" clamp** deserves the same caution with wrapping the shaft, as you do with the metal clamp. Again, when you tighten the clamp with the triangular connector, use only enough pressure to keep the tension on the rubber band. When you place the clamp over the tip, you will pull down with this style of clamp, to put tension on the rubber band, and then pushing down simultaneously while applying pressure, you will push down on the connector, to hold the tension in place. **Do NOT over apply pressure.** You can still scratch and dint your shaft with a plastic clamp. Again, the finishing steps, scuffing, shaping, chalking and re-chalking, remain the same,

3. Using the **pocket pal clamp**, requires the same cautions. However, this clamp goes over the end of the tip and aligns with the shaft in a "U" formation. When you put the "O" ring on and push down, you have a much less chance for any damage to the shaft. Only apply as much pressure as is necessary to hold the tip and the clamp in place.

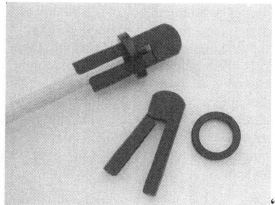

"U"Clamp"

Mr. Porper has also designed a clamping tool for the guy on the road. It is a **Tip Clamp** that allows you to re-apply a tip that might have come off during a match or while you are away from home. You simply sand off the remaining leather on your ferrule, and sand the bottom of the tip. Use the Prik Stik or tip pik, piking the bottom of the tip and then you push the tip into the head of the **Tip Clamp**. Apply gel or glue to the ferrule and insert the shaft into the **Tip Clamp** and push the large part of the clamp down the shaft. When it has dried, push it back up and the tip is ready.

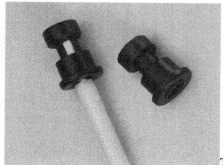

Tip Clamp

Finally, the last method that I wanted to present to you is one used and taught to me by my friend Walter. Walter has been tipping cues over fifty years and uses the same methodology for prepping the ferrule and tip as I do. When he applies the tip with the gel, he holds it in place for the ten seconds to allow it to begin to set. At this point, without clamps or rubber bands of any kind, he attaches the shaft to the stock and turns the entire cue upside down, lets it drop a few inches from the floor, giving the tip a slight tap on the hard floor to be sure there are no air bubbles and places it into a floor or wall rack up side down with the tip receiving pressure from the weight of the cue itself. Or you can put the cue vertical in the corner of a room in the event you do not have a rack at your disposal. Be sure to check that the tip is still aligned after you have tapped it lightly on the floor.

Inversion Technique

Terry Macioge

Caution... If you do not have a floor or wall rack, to keep your cue vertical, use the corner of a room and stand it against the two walls. No clamps are required and gravity does its job. This is a good example of how little pressure must be applied to the tip for it to adhere properly. The weight of the cue itself is all the pressure needed to secure the tip during the drying process. It is important to be sure that the tip has set well enough in the first ten seconds, so that once the cue is turned over, the tip does not slip off center and dry in a position that would require you to start the procedure over from scratch.

It is understood that the cue must remain untouched and perfectly vertical in order for this process to work effectively. The advantage is no clamps are required and the technique is very successful and safe. No damage to your shaft.

The Clean Up

When the clamping and gluing process has been completed, you might have some cleaning up to do. It is quite possible that some glue or dyes from the tip may have gotten on the ferrule and cleaning or sanding may be required. I have my own methods of doing this and use products that I dare not mention to you. I cannot give all my secrets away. I will say that a good Shark Oil or Q Cleaning solution is a product that you should have on hand to remove excess chalk and residues from the shafts and ferrule. Sand paper of a high grit number like 400 and above will remove and clean the ferrule. I take a small sheet of sand paper and cut it into four sections about 4" X4" in size. Cupping the paper in the palm of my hand, I take the shaft only, and wrap the sand paper around the ferrule. Then, while holding the tip facing the floor, starting with the connecting joint, I stroke the shaft lightly to remove anything that might be on the shaft. I stroke forward towards the tip and never stroke back n forth, only one direction. After stroking the shaft a few strokes and making sure it is clean, I will move forward to concentrate on the ferrule and with a rotating motion. I continue to use very short strokes, to polish the ferrule. Always sanding in one direction from the back of the ferrule toward the tip. As you reach the tip with each stroke forward, it is important

90

to open your hand and let the excess residues fall to
the stroke again from the bottom side of the ferrule
your hand around the ferrule and as you stroke rot
hand. This will give a smooth even finish all around the ...

By the time you have shaped and cut your tip so that you have a
perfect arc on top, you most likely have removed the coating on the
side of the tip as well. If it bothers you, a trick that a lot of guys use is
to take a permanent marker and before you start your finish sanding
process on the ferrule, use the marker to color the sides of the tip. If
you prefer, you can purchase Joe Porper's Tip Touchup, a liquid
leather burnisher, to coat and strengthen the side of the tip. Most guys
use a plain black marker to recoat the tip and darken the leather.

there you have it. Now it was not that bad, was it?

I hope I was able to provide the information that many of you have requested of me for so long and that you may have learned a few pointers. A couple things I would like to mention about cue care:

1. Do not to leave your cue in your car. Change of temperatures can cause havoc with your cue and possibly cause the cue to warp on you. Remember, cues are made of wood and wood breathes. It expands and contacts with hot and cold variations of temperature.

2. Never lean your cue against a wall for long periods of time, as you are playing pool or lay it on a table with the tip on the rail while the butt is on the table or visa versa. This leaning or placing your cue on an uneven surface can also cause a cue to warp. It certainly does not do it any good.

3. If a wall or floor rack are not available to place your cue in an upright position, there are special table cue clamps that can be purchased for 2, 4, 6 cues, that will keep your cue vertical. I recommend laying your cue flat on the pool table so that the entire cue is on the table bed, if your pool playing has ended, for the day. Treat your cue with TLC and it will perform for you like it was designed.

4. Whether you live in a home where your pool table is at ground level, or you reside in an area of the country where you might have a basement or finished recreational room below the earth's surface, and you want to place a wall rack on the wall, never place it on the exterior wall of the house. Always choose an interior wall for hanging your cue rack. The reason is because the exterior walls are cooler than the interiors, you could end up with a cool wall on the outside while the temperature on the inside, especially during winter months, when the furnaces are on, will be warmer. This would have the front of the cue facing heat while the back of the cue would be receiving cooler air from an outside or underground wall. These temperature variances can cause a cue shaft to warp. I experienced this in a retail store I was managing and all our cue racks happened to be on an exterior cinderblock wall.

Very poorly insulated, I might add. During the winter months the exterior wall was cold, and the heat was on in the interior. Needless to say, it could be a costly error, especially if you have valuable cues on your wall racks.

I have provided the information and techniques necessary for you to be able to change the tip on your cue. **Just have confidence in your self and doing it and you will succeed**.

Terry Macioge

Summary

As a novice, you should be feeling a little more confident now about your cue and how to replace its tip. Hopefully, you have learned a few things by reading these pages.

We covered a lot of material in a few chapters including the different types of tools that can be beneficial to maintaining the shape of your cue tip. We also covered the different types of ferrules that are found on different cues, and some of the many types of tips that are used by players. Finally, we covered six ways to anchor the tip through the use of several types of clamps, rubber band and one method with no clamps at all.

Let us review ... **Ten steps to tipping the cue**

1. **Select the tip... you choose the density.**
2. **Sand the bottom...pik the bottom.**
3. **Remove the old tip...remove/grind away the excess leather.**
4. **Check the ferrule for flatness, and any chips or cracks.**
5. **Apply minimal amount of gel/glue.**
6. **Swirl the gel/glue on the ferrule top...align the tip.**
7. **Clamp the tip...or invert the cue.**
8. **Shape the tip...develop the arc...pik the top...raise the nap**
9. **Chalk...seat the chalk...Re-chalk...Tap off excess.**
10. **Test the Cue...2-3 rails.**

Here are some choices for you to make. What kind of tools do you think you will feel comfortable using in maintaining the tip of your cue? There are plenty of styles of Shapers, Tip Piks, Burnishers, Scuffers and cutting tools to choose from. Can you feel confident about changing your own tip, instead of paying someone else, to do it for you? Hopefully, the pictures and information provided, and the various methods, will give you enough information, to be successful, at changing your own tip. The more times you attempt to replace your tip, the better you will be. If you forget a step, just refer to Chapter IV of the book and you will be fine.

I wish you success, in your efforts, to replacing your first tip.

Directory

-Catalog Sources

-Billiard Parlors

-Retail Stores

-Cue Makers

Terry Macioge

DIRECTORY

SOURCES FOR CUE TIPPING EQUIPMENT

CATALOG SUPPLIERS

Supplier / Address	E-Mail /Fax/Phone
1. Mueller's Recreational Products	1-800-925-7665 Service
4825 South 16th Street	1-800-627-8888 Sales
Lincoln, NE 68512	www.poolndarts.com
2. Saunier-Wilhem Company	1-800-284-5751
114 Gallery Drive	1-724-969-4350
McMurray, PA. 15317	Fax 1-724-969-4354
	info@swcbilliards.com
	www.swcbilliards.com
3. Saunier-Wilhem Company	1-205-854-2822
1605 Center Point Road	Fax 1-205-854-2823
Birmingham, AL 35215	1-800-548-7404

Terry Macioge

4. Saunier-Wilhem Company   1-336-272-3412

   2707 South Elm–Eugene St.   Fax 1-336-272-9794

   Greensboro, NC 27406   1-800-684-2404

INTERNET WEBSITES

Supplier / Address   E-Mail /Fax/Phone

1. Atlas Billiard Supplies   1-800-283-7845

   3721 W. Chase Avenue   Fax 1-847-674-1723

   Skokie, IL 60076-4008   Outside US 1-847-674-1234

    info@cuestik.com

2. Billiards Depot   1-303-664-0684

   P O Box 777   info@billiardsdepot.com

   Louisville, CO 80027

3. Billiards Express   1-800-540-1761

   9800 Hosier Street   Fax 1-757-599-3365

   Newport News, VA 23601   http://www.billiardsexpress.com

4. Billiard Warehouse   1-888-809-POOL

   740 Bennett Mills Road   1-732-833-8012

   Jackson, NJ 08527   Fax 1-413-208-1384

    Sales@billiardwarehouse.com

5. Billiard Zone

   154 Hogsback Road

   Oxford, CT 06478

1-800-517-8889

203-881-5964 local/fax

Sales@billiard-zone.com

6. Classic Cues

   4 Prospect Hill Road

   East Windsor, CT 06088

1-860-627-8494

www.classiccues.com

7. Creative Inventions

   9142-44 Jordan Avenue

   Chatsworth, CA 91311

1-800-388-5132

1-818-727-7966

Fax 1-818-727-9076

www.porper.com/accessories

8. Cue Sight Technologies

   1809 Kilmonack Ln

   Charlotte, NC 28270

   www.billiardsstore.com

   www.poolcuestore.com

1-877-283-7444

Fax 1-704-321-1992

1-704-821-1010

Sales@cuesight.com

http://www.cuesight.com

9. Mueller's Recreational Products

   4825 South 16th Street

   Lincoln, NE 68512

1-800-925-7665 Service

1-800-627-8888 Sales

www.poolndarts.com

10. Play Pool   1-262-502-9354

    PO Box 716   Fax 1-262-502-9361

    Milwaukee, WI 53201   webmaster@playpool.com10

11. Pool Cue Discount store   1-800-721-1071

    1280 South River Oaks Drive   Sales@abcstore.com

    Blackshear, GA 31516

12. Seybert's Billiard Supply   1-877-314-2837

    702 E. Chicago road   1-517-279-7585

    Coldwater, MI 49036   Fax 1-517-279-8765

                             seyberts@cbpu.com

13. Thompson Sporting goods, Inc 1-800-707-1901

    400 Arnold Street   Fax 1-912-882-0842

    Kingsland, GA 31548   tsg@tds.net

14. Walt's Billiard Supplies   1-352-625-5661

    10313 E. Hwy 40   cyberpockets@yahoo.com

    Silver springs, FL 34488
http://store.yahoo.com/waltsbilliards

FROM THE PUBLISHER OF "BILLIARDS DIGEST," LUBY PUBLISHING, INC., BILLIARD PARLORS AND RETAIL STORES SELLING THE "BILLIARD DIGEST AND CUE SUPPLIES

UNITED STATES

Anchorage Billiard Palace, 3707 Woodland Drive #4, Anchorage, AK

Jones Bros. Pool Tables, 309 West Broadway, North Little Rock, AR

Break-N-Run Billiards, 3418 Nettleton, Jonesboro, AR

Pockets, Inc, 1062 S. Wilmot, Tucson, AZ

Boodink's Billiard Pro Shop, 7700 S. Priest Dr., Tempe, AZ

Hard Times Billiards, 17450 Bellflower Blvd., Bellflower, CA

Quality Billiards of San Diego, 930 W. Washington, Suite 1, San Diego, CA

East Street Billiards, 511 Tyler Street, Monterey, CA

Hot Shots Billiards, 250 Pomeroy Avenue, Pismo Beach, CA

California Billiards Club, 881 E. El Camino Real, Mountain View, CA

Shoreline Billiards, 1400 N. shoreline Blvd., Mountain View, CA

The Broken Rack, 6005 Shellmound, Emeryville, CA

Pacific Billiards, 819-A Street, Suite 26, San Rafael, CA

Slo Billiards, 1987 Santa Barbara St., San Luis Obispo, CA

Danny K's Billiards, 1096 Main Street, Orange, CA

Italian Trade Commision, 1801 Avenue of the Stars, Suite 700, Los Angeles, CA

Olhausen Billiards, 5620 B Kearney Mesa Road, San Diego, CA

Shakespeare's, 2375 15th Street, Denver, CO

Showcase Billiards, 12301 N. Tejon St. NO. 202B, Westminister, CO

Crown Billiards, 264 S. Frontage Rd., New London Shopping Ctr., New London, CT

Boston Billiard Club, 20 Backus Avenue, Danbury, CT.

Boston Billiard Club, 111 Black Rock Turnpike, Fairfield, CT

Rack N Roll Billiards, 268 Atlantic Street, Stamford, CT

Q Stix Billiards, 213 Newark Shopping Ctr., Newark, DE

The Billiard Factory, 5585 University Blvd, West Jacksonville, FL

Dr. G's School of Pool, 2813 S. Hiawassee Rd. STE 207, Orlando, FL

Starbuck's Billiards, 22 Palafox Place, Pensacola, FL

Break Time, 519 Jones Avenue, Haines City, FL

Starcade Billiards Inc., 34 Eglin Parkway S.E., Ft. Walton Beach, FL

Kisshot Billiard, 201 N. US 1, Jupiter, FL

West Coast Billiards, 6801 4th Street North, St.Petersburg, FL

Sidepockets, 9666 Leeward Avenue, Largo, FL

Livingstons Billiards, 6239 14th St. West, Bradenton, FL

Kue & Karom Billiards Sales, 1860 A Northgate Blvd, Sarasota, FL

The Pool House, 6259 Peachtree Industrial, Atlanta, GA

Murphy's Brass Rail, 1120 Mitchell Bridge Road, Athens, GA

Barley's Billiards, 338 Peachtree St. NE, Atlanta, GA

Hawaiian Brian's Billiards Pro Shop, 1680 Kapiolani Blvd., Honolulu, HI

AM-PRO Sports, 96-1243 Waihona Street, Pearl City, HI

The Green Room, 111 S Lincoln Way, North Aurora, IL

Dixie Billiard Equipment, 15407 S. Cicero Avenue, Oak Forest, IL

Pockets, 4034 fox Valley Ctr. Drive, Aurora, IL

The Green Room, 224 W. Ogden, Downers Grove, IL

Chris's Billiards, 4637 N. Milwaukee Avenue, Chicago, IL

Red Shoes Billiards, 12009 S. Pulaski Road, Alsip, IL

Bowling & Billiard Center, Illinois State University, Normal, IL

Starship Billiards Parlor, 2301 Stevenson Drive, Springfield, IL

Quentin corner Pocket, 755 N. Quentin Road, Palatine, IL

Cue-N-You Billiards, 1858 E. Belvidere, Grayslake, IL

Cue Time Billiards, 3910 S. Harlem Avenue, Lyons, IL

Terry Macioge

Shapes Bar & Billiards, 1504 N. Naper Blvd., Naperville, IL

Classic Billiard Inc, 1701 N. Larkin, Crest Hill, IL

City Pool Hall, 640 W. Hubbard, Chicago, IL

Walnut Ridge Pool N Patio, 720 E. HWY 131, Clarksville, IN

Jay Orner Billiard Co., 6333 Rockville Road, Indianapolis, IN

C & C Billiards, Inc., 2110 N. Meridian St. Indianapolis, IN

Cue and Billiard Showcase, 7940 Pendleton Pike, Indianapolis, IN

Steepleton's, 927 Broadway, Louisville, KY

Jillian's Entertainment, 1387 S. 4th Street, Louisville, KY

Rack 66, Inc., 5004 Preston Hwy, Louisville, KY

Cue Time, 532 Three Springs Road, Bowling Green, KY

Two Sisters Billiards, 960 I-10 Service Road, Slidell, LA

Sticks Billiards, 3220 Johnston Street, Lafayette, LA

Corner Pocket Billiards, 2424 Williams Blvd., Kenner, LA

Boston Billiard Club, 885 Riverdale Street, West Springfield, MA

Snookers Billiard Club Ltd, 1791 Boston Road, Springfield, MA

BC's Billiards & Darts, 242 W. Main Street, Avon, MA 02322

Boston Billiard Club, 126 Brookline Avenue, Boston, MA

Pocket Family Billiards, 28 Arnold Street, New Bedford, MA

Fast Break Billiards, 15 Messenger Street, Plainville, MA

Eight Ball Billiard Parlor, 1585 Hancock Street, Quincy, MA

B.C. S Billiard & Darts, 242 West Main Street, Avon, MA

Good Darts, Ltd., 2134 B Generals Hwy, Annapolis, MD

Charlie's Pro Shop, 2401 G North Point Blvd., Baltimore, MD

The Billiard Club, 2440 Churchville Road, Belair, MD

B & W Billiards, 2830 Pinegrove Avenue, Port Huron, MI

All State Darts & Billiards, 14349 Telegraph Road, Redford, MI

Pockets of Michigan, 1618 S Washington, Lansing, MI

Ball & Cue Billiards & Pro Shop, 3434 Fort Street, Lincoln Park, MI

Hall of Fame Billiards, 5775 E. 13 Mile Road, Warren, MI

Mr. Grumpy's Billiards, 1618 S. Washington Avenue, Lansing, MI

Al's Billiards, 1319 W Larpenter, Roseville, MN

Shooters Billiards & Pro Shop, 1934 E Highway 13, Burnsville, MN

Billiard Street Café, 7178 University Avenue NE, Fridley, MN

Checkers Billiards Bar & Grill, 3606 W Division Street, St. Cloud, MN

Doc's Bohemian Cue, Inc., 8465 Plaza Blvd., Spring Lake Park, MN

Farmington Billiards, 933 8th Street, Farmington, MN

G & G Haus of Billiards and Darts, 3560 S Campbell, Springfield, Mo

Schmidt Billiards, 2525 Bernadette Square, Columbia, MO

Lacy's Tavern, 4586 Clinton Blvd., Jackson, MS

Art's Billiard Supply, 17801 E. 39th Street, Independence, MT

Jillians, 200 E. Bland Street, Charlotte, NC

Brass Tap and Billiards, 3316 "O" Capital Blvd., Raleigh, NC

Babineau's, 1102 Buck Jones Road, Raleigh, NC

County Retreat Billiards, 90221 Hwy 105, South Boone, NC

Tom's Q-Stix, 4700 Dudley, Lincoln, NE

Boston Billiard Club, 55 Northeastern Blvd., Nashua, NH

Phila-American Shuffleboard Co., 200 West Clinton Avenue, Oaklyn, NJ

Billiards on the Green, 6701 Blackhorse Pike Cardiff Plaza, Egg Harbor Twp., NJ

Comet Billiards, 233 Littleton Road, Parsippany, NJ

Ocean County Library, 101 Washington Street, Toms River, NJ

Mission Billiards, 221 10th Street, Alamogordo, NM

Billiard World, Inc., 5411 W Charleston Blvd., Las Vegas, NV

Billiard Factory of Nevada, Inc., 4254 E Charleston Blvd., Las Vegas, NV

A-1 Billiards, 1616 E Charleston, Las Vegas, NV

Corner Billiards, 85 Fourth Avenue, New York, NY

Soho Billiards, 298 Mulberry Street, New York NY

Amsterdam Billiard Club, 344 Amsterdam Avenue, New York, NY

Amsterdam Billiard Club, 210 E 86th Street (Between 2nd & 3rd) New York, NY

Fieldstone Recreation Center, 5905 Broadway, Bronx, NY

Bayridge Billiards, 505 Covington Avenue, Brooklyn, NY

The Pocket Billiard Lounge, 33 W State Street, Binghamton, NY

Sir Billiards, Inc., 20 Lock Street, Lockport, NY

Bogie's Billiards, 8216 Main Street, Williamsville, NY

Carom Café, 34-02 Linden Place, Flushing, NY

House of Billiards, 3660 Delaware Avenue, Tonawanda, NY

Six Pockets Billiard Café, Ridge Hudson Plaza, 715 E Ridge Road, Rochester, NY

4-Ever Billiards, 4231 Mahoning Avenue, Youngstown, OH

Sharks-N-shooters Poolroom, 11952 Hamilton Avenue, Cincinnati, OH

Suzi-Cue Pool Hall, 1950 North 4th, Columbus, OH

Tech Novelty Inc., 7723 Southwick Drive, Dublin, OH

Sharky's of Brookside, 3415 S. Peoria Avenue, Tulsa, OK

Tulsa Billiard Palace Ltd, E 8155A East 21Street, Tulsa, OK

Pool Tables Etc., 36 W Memorial, Oklahoma City, OK

Hot Shots Billiards, 4900 SW Western Avenue, Beaverton, OR

Cue Ball, 1262 State Street, Salem, OR

McGill's Billiard Academy, 1306 NW Hoyt Street B-1, Portland, OR

Foxy's Billiards, 1104 Claire Drive, Birdsboro, PA

Gebhardt Bowling Supply, 1010 Airport Road, Allentown, PA

Drexeline Billiards, 5100 State Road, Drexel Hill, PA

Club Med Billiards, 13 Kelso Street, Harrisburg, PA

Alpha Billiards Club, 54 Garrett Road, Upper Darby, PA

Pool City, Inc., No.4 Old Clariton Road, Pittsburgh, PA

Classic Billiards, 275 Schuylkill Rd. (Rt23), Phoenixville, PA

American Billiards, 295California Rd., Quakertown, PA

Royal Billiards, 2622 Bethlehem Pike, Hatfield, PA

D & L Billiards, 377 Atwells Avenue, Providence, RI

Boston Billiard Club, 33 Lambert Lind Hwy, Warwick, RI

Snookers, 145 Clifford Street, Providence, RI

Charleston Billiards & Cue Co., 7685 Northwoods Blvd., Charleston, SC

The Marble Club, 2315 Mt. Rushmore Road, Rapid City, SD

High Pocket Inc, 5099 Old Summer, Memphis, TN

8-Ball Billiard & Dart Supply, 5854 Jacksboro Hwy, Ft Worth, Tx-*

Texas Billiard Supply, 1417 San Eduardo, Laredo, TX

JD's Billiards, 105-A EXP 83, Pharr, TX

The Billiard Factory, 15705 San Pedro, San Antonio, TX

Legends Billiards & Grill, 100 W. Main, Brenham, TX

International Billiards, 2311 Washington Avenue, Houston, TX

Breaktime Billiards, 460-A S Commerce Avenue, Front Royal, VA

The Playing Field, 7801 W Broad Street, Richmond, VA

Q-Masters Billiards Restaurant & Showroom, 5612-A Princess Anne Road, Virginia Beach, VA

Long's Billiard Supply, 9908 Warwick Blvd., Newport News, VA

Obelisk Billiard Club, 14346 Warwick Blvd., Suite 348, Newport News, VA

Todd's Cue & Pro Shop, 2125 Staples Mill Road, Richmond, VA

R&J Amusement Co, 249 Blue Ridge Drive, Orange, VA

Classic Billiards, Inc., 2817 Wheaton Way, Bremerton, WA

MCQ's Billiards, 9416 E Sprague, Spokane, WA

Sure Shot Billiards & Darts, 5510 W Clearwater, Kennewick, WA

Brunswick Billiards, 8663 196th Avenue, Bristol, WI

Terry Macioge

Memorial Student Recreation Center, 302 10th Avenue, Menomonie, WI

Viking Cue Mfg., 2710 Syene Road, Madison, WI

Top Shots, 135 ½ S. 4th, Lacrosse, WI

CANADA

Great White Billiards, 100-8228 Macleod Trail, SE, Calgary, Alberta

Stix Billiard Club, 420 5255 Richmond Rd. SW, Calgary, Alberta

"The Dogs" Billiard Sales, 9808 100th Avenue, Grand Prairie, Alberta

Palason Billiards, Inc., 2363 43 E. Avenue, Lachine, Quebec

The Corner Pocket, C-1 2310 50 Avenue, Red Deer, Alberta

Rack-Em-Up Billiards, 1916 Pitt Street North, Cornwall, Ontario

Cue Manufacturers

For a list of cue manufacturers you can refer to

- **"Blue Book of Pool Cues" by Brad Simpson**
- **"The Pool Cue Book" by Stephen Mayhew**
- **Billiard Congress of America's website, www.bca.com**

BIBLIOGRAPHY

Billiard Congress of America
"Billiards: The Official Rules and Records Book
1700 South 1st Avenue
Iowa City, Iowa 52240
1-319-351-2112
Fax 1-319-351-7767

"Byrne's New Standard Book of Pool and Billiards"
By Robert Byrnes
Harcourt Brace & Company, Trade Publishers
525 B Street
San Diego, CA 92101

"Mueller Recreational Products"
4825 South 16th Street
Lincoln, NE 68512
1-800-925-7665 Customer Service
1-800-627-8888 Sales
E-mail: info@poolndarts.com
Website: www.poolndarts.com

"The Complete Idiot's Guide to Pool and Billiards"
By Ewa Mataya Laurance
Alpha Books
1633 Broadway, 7th Floor
New York, New York 10019-6785
p.46

Terry Macioge

"The New Illustrated Encyclopedia of Billiards"
By Mike Shamos
The Lyons Press
123 West 18th Street
New York, New York 10011
Page 259-260